£19 95·

The Police
of France

Calais
Dunkerque
PAS-DE-CALAIS
Boulogne-sur-Mer
St-Omer
Lille
NORD
Béthune
Montreuil
Lens
Douai Valenciennes
ARDENNES
SOMME
Arras
Cambrai
Avesnes-s/Helpe
MEUSE
Abbeville
Péronne
St-
Charleville-Mézières
Cherbourg
Dieppe
Amiens
Quentin
AISNE
Sedan
MEURTHE-ET-MOSELLE
Le Havre
Montdidier
Vervins
Rethel
Vouziers
MOSELLE
MANCHE
SEINE-MME
Beauvais
OISE
Laon
Reims
Verdun
Briey
Thionville
Forbach
Bayeux
Rouen
Compiègne
Soissons
Ste-
Boulay
Sarreguemines
Caen
Les Andelys
Clermont
Chau
Menehould
Metz
Wissembourg
St-Lô
CALVADOS
Évreux
Senlis
Château-
Thierry
MARNE
M. Bar-le-D.
Chau-
Salins
Nancy
Haguenau
Coutances
Bernay
EURE
Meaux
Épernay
Châl-s/-
Commercy
Toul
Lunéville
BAS-RHIN
Vire
Argentan
Dreux
PARIS
SEINE-
Provins
Vitry-le-F.
St-Dizier
Neufchâteau
St-Dié
Saverne
Strasbourg
Morlaix
St-Malo
Avranches
Mortagne-au-P
EURE-
Chartres
Nogent-
ET-
Troyes
Molsheim
Lannion
St-Brieuc
Dinan
Fougères
ORNE
Mayenne
le-R
AUBE
Bars/-
Chaumont
Langres
Sélestat-Erstein
Ribeauvillé
Brest
Guingamp
Pontivy
CÔTES-DU-NORD
ILLE-ET-
Laval
MAYENNE
Mamers
Vendôme
SARTHE
Le Mans
ET-LOIR
Nogent-s/S
Sens
MARNE
HTE
Vesoul
Colmar
HAUT-RHIN
FINISTÈRE
Châteaulin
Rennes
Segré
La Flèche
Pithiviers
Montargis
YONNE
Lure
Thann
Mulhouse
Quimper
MORBIHAN
VILAINE
Châteaubriant
Chau
Gontier
LOIR
Orléans
LOIRET
Montbard
CÔTE-D'OR
Belfort
TERRE-DE-BELFORT
Lorient
Vannes
Redon
Angers
MAINE
Blois
Auxerre
Dijon
Montbéliard
Besançon
St-Nazaire
Ancenis
Tours
INDRE-
ET-LOIRE
Romorantin-L
Avallon
Dole
DOUBS
LOIRE-
ATLANTIQUE
Nantes
Cholet
Saumur
ET-CHER
CHER
Clamecy
Autun
JURA
Pontarlier
Loches
Issoudun
Bourges
NIÈVRE
Beaune
Lons-le-Saunier
Chinon
St-Amand-
Chalon-s/S
La Roche-s/-Yon
Bressuire
Châtellerault
INDRE
Nevers
Montrond
SAÔNE-ET-L.
St-Claude
HTE-
VENDÉE
Parthenay
Poitiers
La Châtre
Châteauroux
Charolles
Louhans
Gex
SAVOIE
Les Sables-d'Olonne
Fontenay-le-Comte
DEUX-
SÈVRES
VIENNE
Le Blanc
Moulins
Mâcon
Bourg-en-B.
St-Julien-en-Genevois
Thonon-les-Bains
Niort
Montmorillon
Montluçon
ALLIER
Vichy
RHÔNE
AIN
Nantua
La Rochelle
St-Jean-d'Angély
Guéret
Bellac
HTE-
CREUSE
Riom
Roanne
Villefranche-s/S
Belley
Annecy
CHARENTE-MARITIME
Confolens
VIENNE
Aubusson
PUY-DE-DÔME
Thiers
Lyon
La Tour-du-Pin
Albertville
Rochefort
Cognac
CHARENTE
Rochechouart
Ussel
Clermont-
Montbrison
LOIRE
Vienne
Chambéry
Saintes
Angoulême
Limoges
F.
Ambert
St-Ét.
ISÈRE
SAVOIE
St-Jean-de-Maurienne
Lesparre-Médoc
Nontron
DORDOGNE
CORRÈZE
Brioude
HTE-
Yssingeaux
Blaye
Jonzac
Tulle
Mauriac
LOIRE
Tournon
Grenoble
Libourne
Périgueux
Brive-la-Gaillarde
CANTAL
St-Flour
Le Puy-
Briançon
GIRONDE
Sarlat-la-C
Gourdon
Figeac
Aurillac
LOZÈRE
Privas
Valence
ALPES-
Bordeaux
Bergerac
LOT
Mende
ARDÈCHE
DRÔME
Gap
HTES-
Langon
Villeneuve-s/-Lot
Largentière
Nyons
HT-PROVENCE
Marmande
Villefranche-de-R.
Rodez
Die
Barcelonnette
LOT-ET-GARONNE
Cahors
TARN-ET-
Alès
Carpentras
Digne
ALPES-
Nérac
Agen
GARONNE
AVEYRON
Le Vigan
GARD
VAUCLUSE
Forcalquier
MARITIMES
Mont-de-Marsan
LANDES
Castelsarrasin
Montauban
Millau
Lodève
VAUCLUSE
Avignon
Castellane
MONACO
Condom
GERS
Albi
TARN
Nîmes
Apt
Nice
Dax
Montpellier
Arles
Aix-en-P.
VAR
Grasse
Bayonne
Mirande
Auch
Toulouse
HÉRAULT
Istres
Draguignan
Oloron-Ste-Marie
Pau
Tarbes
GARONNE
Castres
BOUCHES-DU-RHÔNE
Brignoles
Muret
Carcassonne
Béziers
Marseille
Toulon
PYRÉNÉES-ATLANTIQUES
Argelès-Gazost
Bagnères-de-Bigorre
St-Gaudens
Pamiers
AUDE
Narbonne
HTES-PYRÉNÉES
St-Girons
Foix
Limoux
ARIÈGE
Perpignan
Prades
Céret
PYRÉNÉES-ORIENTALES

VAL-
Pontoise
D'OISE
Mantes-la-Jolie
Montmorency
St-Germain-en-Laye
Argenteuil
Versailles
YVELINES
Palaiseau
Évry
Rambouillet
ESSONNE
Étampes

SEINE-ST-DENIS
HAUTS-
Bobigny
Nanterre
Paris
Le Raincy
DE-SEINE
Nogent-s/M
Boulogne-Bill.
L'Hay-les-Roses
VAL-
Créteil
Antony
DE-MARNE

limite de département
chef-lieu de département
chef-lieu d'arrondissement

HAUTE-CORSE
Calvi
Bastia
Corte
CORSE-DU-SUD
Ajaccio
Sartène

The Police of France

Philip John Stead

MACMILLAN PUBLISHING COMPANY
A Division of Macmillan, Inc.
NEW YORK

Collier Macmillan Publishers
LONDON

Copyright © 1983 by Macmillan Publishing Company
A Division of Macmillan, Inc.

Macmillan Publishing Company
A Division of Macmillan, Inc.
866 Third Avenue, New York, N. Y. 10022

Collier Macmillan Canada, Inc.

Library of Congress Catalog Card Number: 83–5455

Printed in the United States of America

printing number
1 2 3 4 5 6 7 8 9 10

Library of Congress Cataloging in Publication Data

Stead, Philip John.
    The police of France.

    Bibliography: p.
    Includes index.
    1. Police—France—History.   I. Title.
HV8203.S69 1983   363.2'0944   83–5455
ISBN 0-02-930820-8

For
Lucien Durin
Commissaire divisionnaire honoraire de la Police Nationale
in token of
the author's admiration and gratitude

Contents

Contents

Acknowledgments

I am indebted to Dr. Gerald W. Lynch, President of John Jay College of Criminal Justice in the City University of New York, and to Professor Lloyd W. Sealy, my Chairman, and my colleagues in the Department of Law, Police Science and Criminal Justice Administration, for granting me the sabbatical leave that enabled me to complete this book.

My thanks are also due to my former superiors at the British Home Office and to the successive Commandants of the Police Staff College, Bramshill, England, under whom I had the honor of serving: the late Brigadier P.D.W. Dunn; Major General R.W. Jelf; the late Mr. Sydney Lawrence; the late Mr. J.S.H. Gaskain; Sir Colin Woods; Mr. John C. Alderson; and Mr. J.F. Walker, for allowing me to undertake research and teaching in France and to lecture on police topics at British, Canadian, and American universities and police training establishments.

I have happy and grateful memories of the *Ecole Nationale Supérieure de Police,* where successive Directors, Deputy Directors, and Faculty members, Messieurs Henri Baudry, P.-H. Pagès, Roger Lafontaine, Lucien Durin, Paul Marquet, Jean Montreuil ("*le marquis*"), Claude Godard, Maurice Servoz, Henri Souchon and Jean Viple, high-ranking officers of the police, always made me welcome as a teacher and a colleague. I am also grateful to Monsieur Philippe Callet, until recently in charge of the Prefecture of Police's training system, and to Monsieur Jean Confida, formerly a high official in the Prefecture of Police's administration, for their unfailing and generous help.

I am much obliged to Professor Sir Leon Radzinowicz, Professor A.E. Anton and Mr. David Watts Pope for permission to quote from their work.

As regards the literature of the subject, my principal and long-standing indebtedness is to the authoritative writings of two distinguished police officers, Messieurs Henry Buisson and Marcel Le Clère. The bibliography and references in the text will, I hope, indicate the extent of the assistance that their and others' books have given me.

The Police
of France

CHAPTER 1

Government and Police in France

The Governmental Structure

"France is a Republic, indivisible, secular, democratic and social. It shall ensure the equality of all citizens before the law, without distinction of origin, race or religion." So reads the Constitution of the present state of France, the Fifth Republic.

The Republic is governed by a president, elected for seven years, who appoints the prime minister and on the prime minister's proposal, the other members of the government. The government is responsible to Parliament, which is composed of the National Assembly, elected by direct suffrage, and the Senate, elected by indirect suffrage, ensuring representation of the territorial units of the Republic. All laws must be passed by Parliament.

The president is responsible for seeing that the Constitution is respected, for ensuring the regular functioning of the governmental authorities, and for the continuance of the state. The prime minister directs the operation of the government, is responsible for national defense, and ensures the execution of the laws. He may delegate certain of his powers to ministers: thus, the busi-

1

ness of the execution of the laws is largely left to the Minister of Justice and to the Minister of the Interior, head of the civil police, the Police Nationale, and the Minister of Defense, under whose administration is the military police, the Gendarmerie Nationale.

The fact that France has a single system of codified law and a single system of administration of justice (similar in respect of a unitary legal system and a unitary structure of courts to England, but very different indeed from the state of affairs produced by the federal, state, and local systems of the United States) simplifies the standardization of the French police.

The administration of France is of a centralized and uniform character. In Paris is the government of the day, with the bureaucracies that carry out its policies and control the continuing business of the nation. The Civil Service in France, the permanent staff of the administration, is more powerful than the Civil Service in Britain, where local governments recruit their own personnel, known as local government officers, and very much more powerful than in the United States, where the term "civil service" is applied to personnel recruited at state, county, and other levels of local government, the federal civil service weighing far less heavily in the power scale than its local counterparts. In France, the civil servant, the virtually irremovable functionary of the central government, is found everywhere.

France is divided into ninety-six territorial areas known as departments. Each of these is divided into *arrondissements* (districts), of which there are over three hundred in all, and in each *arrondissement* is a number of communes (municipalities), in all over 36,000. A commune may be a very large urban center or a very small country town, but in any case it will have an elected mayor and council, the mayor representing the central government in one aspect and the government of the neighborhood in the other.

In each department is stationed a Commissaire of the Republic, with Deputy Commissaires of the Republic in each *arrondissement*. These Commissaires and Deputy Commissaires of the Republic represent the central government and exercise supervision over the mayors. They themselves are very much under the supervision of the Minister of the Interior. For "economies of size," the ninety-six departments are grouped into twenty-two regions, in each of which there is a regional Commissaire of the

Republic, the minister's coordinator of the activities of the departmental Commissaires. The twenty-two regions are grouped into six Zones of Defense for military purposes, in which the chief civil representative is a Prefect. It may be apposite at this point to mention that until 1982 the official now called a Commissaire of the Republic had been known as a Prefect, the change of title signaling the present government's intention to take a less peremptory part in local government affairs.

The Commissaire of the Republic is responsible, among much else, for the maintenance of public order in the department as a whole, the Deputy Commissaire in the *arrondissement,* and the mayor in the commune. In the case of Paris, however, the special needs of France's capital city and largest urban center are recognized by the long-established institution of a Prefect of Police, responsible for the capital's policing. The three largest metropolitan areas in the provinces, centered on Lyon, Marseille, and Lille, also have a special police regime, a Prefect Delegated for Police being appointed to each of them.

The nature of police has long been the subject of close study and analysis in France. The word "police," indeed, rooted as it is in the Ancient World, in Greece and Rome, first entered the English language in the eighteenth century in its French form.

Civil society has always made rules for its own protection, some of which are in the form of laws, defining and prohibiting antisocial acts and providing for the punishment of those who commit them. One function of police is to take part in enforcing such laws.

Another kind of rule, sometimes in the form of laws, more often takes the form of regulations. Law can only be made by the legislature; regulations are made by administrators in virtue of powers invested in them by law. These regulations the police are required to enforce, thus the same officer may be dealing with an arrested burglar or a greengrocer whose display has encroached on the sidewalk, in the one case enforcing the criminal law and in the other a regulation made perhaps by the mayor of some small town. This regulation-making power is often called "the police power" in France, which is a reminder that until the nineteenth century, the word "police" signified the internal governance of the community. This older notion of police persists, alongside the no-

3

tion of police as personnel and organization, accounting for the much greater part police take in the general administration of France. It is probably true to say that the majority of citizens in the United States and Britain never set foot on police premises, although that majority, alas, is annually diminishing. In France everyone has to go for various individual purposes to the police: for passports, visas, identity cards, driving licenses and other personal and legitimate matters. The police officer, too, is a civil servant, a functionary of the central government, highly visible in all walks of life.

The Police System

The French police system is basically of a dual nature, its two major components being of remarkably different character. Like other European countries, notably Italy, France does not entrust the maintenance of law and order to a single police force or to a single minister.

The older of the two main French police organizations is military, the Gendarmerie Nationale, with over 80,000 officers and other ranks employed in police duties. The other police organization is civil, the Police Nationale, with some 108,000 personnel. The Gendarmerie is under the Minister of Defense, the Police Nationale under the Minister of the Interior. The population of France is about 52 million, so the ratio of police to public is greater than in the United States or in England and Wales (400,000:220 million; 120,000:49 million, respectively). The reasons for this disparity lie partly in the multiplicity of police functions in France, but more particularly in how the police are deployed.

THE GENDARMERIE NATIONALE

The Gendarmerie, premier regiment of the French army, polices by far the greatest part of France, some 95 percent of the national territory. Metropolitan areas with high density of population are few and far between and the more sparsely peopled com-

4

munes, the countryside and the roads, are the province of the Gendarmerie. The communes with less than 10,000 population are policed by the Gendarmerie formations serving in the territorial department concerned. They work at the first level in small units of between five and fifty-five, according to size of their area. There are some four thousand such units, called *brigades* (squads, not to be confused with the higher military formation of the same name), normally stationed in barracks in the main town of the canton. For purposes of administration, they form parts of companies, while companies form parts of groups, and groups are parts of legions. Known as the Departmental Gendarmerie, they operate from fixed points, residing in their duty area, and they constitute the largest component of the force.

The next largest component is the Mobile Gendarmerie, which may be employed anywhere in the country. The business of the Mobile Gendarmerie is the maintenance or restoration of public order. They are riot police, highly trained for their work, and there are 120 squadrons of them, each of 135 officers and other ranks, always ready in the event of trouble. They are deployed on a regional or a departmental basis, motorized, with tanks, armored vehicles, and light aircraft.

The third main formation of the Gendarmerie is the Republican Guard, consisting of a regiment of cavalry and two regiments of infantry, which is always stationed in Paris. The Guard plays a stately and colorful part in the life of the capital, where, among its many duties, is the mounting of guards to protect the president and other high officers of the Republic.

The Gendarmerie operate under the control of their Director-General, who is a civil magistrate. An Inspectorate-General, under a general, reports on the state of the force to the Minister of Defense.

The illusion, harbored by most foreigners, that *all* French police are gendarmes, is surely due to the latter's omnipresence and high visibility for centuries past. The wearing of the *képi,* too, the cap with the almost horizontal visor and the flat round top, by uniformed civil police and Gendarmerie alike, fosters the confusion. But the traveller over French roads, especially if driving a car, is more likely to see a gendarme than any other kind of police officer.

THE POLICE NATIONALE

The national civil police, the Police Nationale, operate mainly in the urban centers with populations of more than 10,000. Under the Minister of the Interior, who has a Director-General of the force in his ministry headquarters, the organization is complex. The Director-General administers the work of the police through headquarters branches.

The administrative requirements of such a large service are obviously very heavy, including as they do the processes of recruitment and training, finance, personal documentation, and the provision of buildings and equipment, the latter involving armament, transportation, communications, and uniforms. The operational aspects at first sight in some cases are readily identifiable with Anglo-American police activities. The Directorate of Urban Police, responsible for the policing of the cities, with its patrol and plain-clothes elements, or the Directorate of Criminal Investigation (*Police judiciaire*), concerned mainly with the regional detective services that operate against serious crime and pursue cases beyond the scope of the city police or Gendarmerie resources: these seem familiar enough, as does the existence of a separate police organization, the Air and Frontier Police, in a country with extensive land frontiers, sea coasts, and incessant air traffic.

Another powerful arm of the French police, however, has no apparent counterpart in either the American or the British police scheme: the Republican Security Companies (*Compagnies républicaines de sécurité*), popularly, or, rather, unpopularly, known as the CRS. These are the civil-police version of the Mobile Gendarmerie, approaching the latter in numbers of personnel, organized in 61 companies of between 210 and 255 officers and men. Their whole style is military, based on barracks, with the officers addressed as if they held army ranks—lieutenant, captain, major, colonel—but they are all civilian functionaries of the same kind as the other members of the Police Nationale. They do not have the heavy armament of the Gendarmerie Mobile but are equally able to move fast to wherever they may be needed, each company being self-sufficient in transportation, communications, and catering. Their business, too, is primarily with the maintenance and restoration of public order, giving the government a numerous and well-trained emergency reserve. As they are a permanent and professional force, they can hardly be compared with the National Guard in the United States.

In the event of public turbulence, therefore, the authorities have over 30,000 men ready to be concentrated on the scene of trouble. There are good historical reasons for this.

Even more alien to police organization in the United States or Britain is the work of the Directorate of General Intelligence and Gambling (*Renseignements généraux et des jeux*), whose business occupies some 2,500 police officers and is tersely summarized in its 1974 charter as being "the search for and centralization of intelligence of a political, social and economic nature necessary for the information of the Government." The main thrust of General Intelligence is in the sphere of public opinion, which it seeks to measure by the collection, collation, and interpretation of data from a wide variety of sources, including the mass media, periodicals, books, statistics, opinion polls, neighborhood gossip, and the infiltration of unions, associations, and other groups. The "line" organization that feeds in the information is on a regional basis, with units at the departmental level.

Equally unidentifiable with regular American or British police practice is the Directorate of Counter-Espionage (*Surveillance du Territoire*, "surveillance of the country," usually referred to in conversation as "the DST"), whose mission is to counter the efforts of foreign agents on French soil to impair the security of France. In the United States this function is performed by the Federal Bureau of Investigation of the Department of Justice and in Britain by the Security Service, "MI 5," a nonpolice organization. The DST is covered by official secrecy and its deployment is not communicated.

THE PREFECTURE OF POLICE OF PARIS

Though the police of Paris is an integral part of the Police Nationale and is therefore under the Director-General at the Ministry of the Interior, since 1800 Paris has had its unique Prefect of Police, an office amply justified by the history of its holders and of the police organization under their command, the

Prefecture of Police, and by the special needs of a city that is the seat of national government, the focal center of administration, the site of numerous embassies and consulates, and a magnet throughout the year for tourists, students, artists, business people, refugees, and increasingly, terrorists and other international predators.

The Prefect of Police commands what is in effect a kind of microcosm of the Police Nationale, with its own bureaucracy, administrative, and operational branches, the latter comprising the uniformed or patrol force, criminal investigation, and general intelligence.

In addition, the Prefect of Police is the Prefect of the Paris Zone of Defense, which confers a certain responsibility for police outside his immediate jurisdiction, in Hauts-de-Seine, Seine-Saint-Denis, and Val-de-Marne, the three territorial departments encircling Paris. Overall, some 31,000 police are at his disposal in his capacity of Defense Zone Prefect.

To assist him, the Prefect has other high officials, members of the élite prefectoral corps of France's administrators, one of whom is Secretary-General of the Defense Zone, a second Secretary-General for the zone's police administration, and a third who is director of his cabinet.

MUNICIPAL POLICE

The French police system is predominantly centralized but, as mentioned above, a certain amount of police responsibility devolves upon the local community in the person of the mayor. In urban centers of over 10,000 population, however, the police power is exercised by the departmental Commissaire of the Republic. The Code of Communal Administration ordains that the mayor of a commune wields the police power under the supervision of the higher administration of the department. The Code lists police areas of mayoral concern, including the safety and convenience of passage on public thoroughfares, attacks on public tranquillity, brawls, disputes, gatherings, mode of conveyance of deceased persons, and road traffic within the commune.

The policing of rural areas of the commune is also the mayor's responsibility, a duty normally performed by the *garde champêtre* (a cross between a rustic policeman and a forest ranger). The *garde champêtre* is appointed by the mayor, with the approval of the Commissaire or Deputy Commissaire of the department.

Gardes champêtres have been a feature of French country life since the Middle Ages. There are about 30,000 of them and they make a considerable contribution to law enforcement. They have police powers not only in connection with hunting and fishing but also with public drunkenness; they can call on the mayor and the commander of the local gendarmerie for assistance, which must be given, and they in turn can be required to assist in police investigations. The presence of so many watchful guardians rich in local knowledge is a valuable police resource, however homely they may appear.

In recent times the mayors of some cities have tended to recruit municipal police, uniformed and armed, to enforce local regulations, even though there are units of the Police Nationale in their communes.

Police and State

The police system outlined above always strikes Americans and Britons as being singularly more powerful than the police systems of their own countries. The numbers and armament of the police, the coexistence of military and civil forces, are highly impressive, as are their legal powers, which will be shown in later chapters. Even more impressive, however, is the fact that so much police power is at the disposal of the central government, the political government of the day. The citizens of the United States and Britain have never seen fit to entrust their governments with such massive police strength.

Accustomed as American and British people are to the idea of localized police, it may also seem strange to them that nearly all police officers in France are either civil functionaries of the central administration or members of the military forces, in either case virtually independent of local political control.

It may seem odd, too, that the high command of the police is not in the hands of professional police officers, as is always the case in Britain and usually the case in the United States. In France the Roman concept of the civil power taking precedence of the force of arms is much in evidence. The Minister of the Interior or the Minister of Defense is in charge of the police, and nationwide, the Commissaires of the Republic and the police Prefects are the dominant police authorities. Police, the French perhaps think (just as war is said to be too serious a matter to be left to soldiers), is too serious a matter to be left to police officers.

In any comparison of French and Anglo-American policing, one must inevitably ask why the central government of France has built up such large public-order maintenance forces and why so much police effort is directed into the gathering of intelligence. The answers to both questions are writ large in the history of France.

England had a civil war and a revolution in the seventeenth century; America had a revolution in the eighteenth century and a civil war in the nineteenth. But these events, cataclysmic as they were, do not fall into any subsequent pattern of violent political upheaval. In France it has been otherwise.

After the anarchy of the Fronde in the seventeenth century came the autocratic monarchy of the Bourbons, Louis XIV and his successors. This was destroyed by the Revolution, which began in 1789 and which, after final failure to govern effectively, gave way to the far more autocratic rule of Napoleon I. Disaster in war opened the way for the return of the Bourbons, who were violently overthrown in 1830. A younger branch of the family supplied another king, Louis-Philippe, whose reign lasted until 1848, when revolution engendered the Second Republic. This had a short life; a nephew of the great Napoleon got himself elected president and in 1852 by *coup d'état* transformed the Second Republic into the Second Empire. Military defeat put an end to this adventure, which was followed by the carnage of the civil war of the Paris Commune in 1871. Then came the Third Republic, whose rapid succession of governments, gravely threatened by riots in 1934, ended with the Nazi invasion in 1940. Marshal Pétain's "Vichy" state lasted until 1944, when, after a brief resumption of the Third Republic, the Fourth Republic was inaugurated in 1946. A series of weak coalition governments ended in 1958 with domestic disaffection and the Algerian crisis bringing General de Gaulle to power, with the Fifth Republic. This has survived, though menaced by street rioting in 1968, when the regime almost perished.

With this pattern of constitutional reversals dominating France's political history since 1789, such reversals so often being the consequence of the government's loss of control of the streets, is there any wonder that French statesmen have become intensely conscious of the need to be well informed and to have immediately at hand the means of maintaining order?

How the French police machine has evolved over the years will be studied in the succeeding chapters in order to arrive at an understanding of the French police system today.

CHAPTER 2

The Ancien Regime

THE ANCIEN REGIME, "the Old Order," is the term that came into use after the Revolution to signify the centuries of monarchical rule that ended in 1793 with Louis XVI's death on the scaffold.

During those centuries the monarchy mastered the feudal nobility and established its autocracy. The struggle was long and hard; men do not easily surrender power. The king had to force his way from being first among equals to become the sovereign power of the realm. The medieval baron had been judge and policeman in his own domain, large or small as that domain might be. Might was right and seigneurial jurisdiction was exercised from the castle by the local magnate. Gradually the kings introduced royal judges, called seneschals and bailiffs, into the feudal courts, bringing some semblance of royal order into the local scheme and providing a means of enforcing royal ordinances.

In the early seventeenth century, the principle of associating royal officials with local governance was substantially implemented when Cardinal Richelieu stationed a royal supervisor, the Intendant of Justice, Police, and Finance, in each of the thirty provinces into which France was then divided. This was the genesis of the departmental prefects and of their successors, the departmental Commissaires of the Republic of today.

Even before then, late in the Middle Ages, as the life of cities, which had decayed with the eclipse of the civic order of the Roman Empire, began to be renewed, the kings had found a valuable counterpoise to the power of the landed nobility. The municipalities were encouraged to develop their independence, on a limited scale, and the charters granted to them by the kings gave their governing corporations the right to maintain order within their walls. Thus came into being a kind of municipal police, an essential stage in police development, in which may be seen the genesis of today's urban police units.

By the end of the Middle Ages, the kings had established the principle of a standing army under royal command. Such an army had to have an internal police element for its own better governance, a provost corps, and given the unsettled and dangerous conditions of the age, the king extended the scope of the military police to include the protection of his subjects in the rural areas and along the main roads. These soldier-policemen, under their provosts, played a great part in making the king's government real to his rustic subjects in times that were still feudal. Here may be seen the genesis of the Departmental Gendarmerie of today.

The kings, for the best of all selfish reasons—self-protection and self-enrichment—took a hand in the administration of justice and police in their capital city of Paris. Since A.D. 1032 a royal official, the Provost of the City, had been governor, judge, and police chief there. The Provost of the Merchants, a civic as distinct from a royal administrator, also operated a police service. The monarchy's was by far the more effective. So, when Henri I appointed Stephanus in 1032 (he died six years before the Battle of Hastings, 1066), the genesis of the Prefect of Police of Paris can be discerned.

Much had been accomplished in these tumultuous years, but much, as always, remained to be done. France was prey to great disruption and in Paris, even more than elsewhere, public safety sank to a low level. Medieval police vessels could not contain the new wine of the energies released by the Renaissance. The young King Louis XIV began his reign amid factious strife and squalid danger.

Louis XIV

"You are aware, Sire," wrote Nicolas de La Mare in the dedication of his great work, *La Traité de la police,* addressing Louis XIV, "that the Police of Your Capital, and of the rest of Your Estates, was, like that of ancient Rome, in almost universal disorder when You Yourself took the reins of government." When the young king emerged from tutelage upon the death of his minister, Cardinal Mazarin, in 1661, Paris had indeed reflected the consequences of several decades of war and internecine strife; it was a city of economic woe and riotous disorder, of crime, dirt, epidemic, darkness, and fire. It was in its old and comprehensive sense that La Mare spoke of police; in the same dedication he defines it as, "the handsome order on which the happiness of states depends."

Measures to secure that "handsome order" would be spelled out in the edicts whereby the king set about reforming the policing of his capital. In theory, the police of the city was the responsibility of the Provost of Paris, who had conducted it in practice during the Middle Ages, but since the last decade of the fifteenth century he had been a ceremonial figure whose duties were performed by his deputies, the Lieutenants. Their jurisdictions and those of other authorities had become hopelessly confused and controversial. Louis decided to cut the Gordian knot and make the policing of the city the responsibility of a new magistrate, the Lieutenant of Police.

It was characteristic of the early years of the young monarch's personal rule that the reform of the police was undertaken in an atmosphere of grave reflection and serious debate. The great names of law and statecraft of the era recur in the record of the king's search for the right measures and the right man. Chancellor Séguier held high-level conferences; Colbert, the immensely able minister, and Louvois, reorganizer of France's armies, entered deeply into the deliberations, as did the jurist Lamoignon. The selection of the man to coordinate and direct the new police system was eventually made on the recommendation of Colbert and Louvois.

The king remarked that a very special kind of person was needed for the post. Colbert wrote an exacting job description:

A man of the robe and a man of the sword and, if the doctor's learned ermine must float upon his shoulder, on his foot must ring the strong spur of the knight; he must be unflinching as a magistrate and intrepid as a soldier; he must not pale before the river in flood or plague in the hospitals, any more than before popular uproar or the threats of your courtiers, for it must be expected that the court will not be the last to complain of the useful rigor of a police carried on in the interest of the well-being and security of all.

Louis commented austerely: "I shall submit *myself* to the rulings of this police, and I intend that all shall respect and obey them as I will."

In December 1666, the edict creating the post of Lieutenant of Police enumerated his duties at considerable length. A summary must suffice here.

The holder of the office would have jurisdiction over the security of the city and its environs; over the illicit bearing of arms; over the cleaning of streets and public places; he would give the necessary orders in the event of fire or flood; he would have responsibility for the food supply of the city and for food prices; for the inspection of markets and fairs, hostelries and lodging houses, gambling houses and places of ill repute; he would take cognizance of illicit assemblies, tumults, seditions, and disorders; of the election of masters and wardens of the six merchant guilds, exercising surveillance of the commercial regulations, and indentures of apprenticeship; of weights and measures; of publishing, printing, and bookselling. The surgeons were required to report to him when patients had wounds to be treated. All persons taken *in flagrante delicto* (caught red-handed) in breach of the police ordinances were to be brought before him for judgment. The various police officials and their respective staffs and forces were required to execute his orders. Citizens were required to lend their aid in the physical enforcement of his orders and warrants. The edict summarizes itself: "Police ... consists in ensuring the repose of the public and of individuals, purging the City of all that can cause disorders, bringing about abundance and making everyone live according to his condition and his duty."

The man who was appointed in 1667 to be the first to bear the burden thus defined was Nicolas-Gabriel de La Reynie. Born in

1625 into a legal family, he was destined for the magistracy. He studied law at the University of Toulouse and became an advocate and a judge. During the civil war of the Fronde he remained loyal to the monarchy, taking shelter with the Duc d'Epernon, Governor of the Province of Guyenne, whose Intendant he became. As a reward for his loyalty, he was allowed to purchase a lucrative legal post in Paris and it was as a Crown lawyer that he took part in Chancellor Séguier's conferences on police reform. When the king signed the letters of appointment of the first Lieutenant of Police, he told Colbert to inform La Reynie that "he would not have had the post if I had known a better man or a more hardworking magistrate."

The monarch's confidence proved amply justified. His new police chief would be one of the great administrators in a great administration, taking a salient part in the regeneration of Paris and effectively implementing the king's domestic policy. Voltaire would pay tribute to La Reynie for paving, cleaning, and lighting the streets with lanterns, commenting that most of the great cities of Europe later followed his example but that none equaled it; no city was paved like Paris, even Rome had no street lighting. When La Reynie left office in 1697, Paris had 6,500 lanterns, placed 20 yards apart. Thus, La Reynie struck at two cardinal causes of crime: dirt and darkness.

It was La Reynie, too, who brought some order into building construction by causing houses to be aligned. He built a beautiful and much-needed bridge over the Seine to alleviate the traffic, the Pont-Royal, planted the Champs-Elysées (arguably the finest street in the world) and leveled the Butte Saint-Roch, where the rue des Moulins runs today. He was a great Parisian.

The police manpower at his disposal became substantial. The royal watch force, the *Guet,* was augmented and a new company of guards was created. La Reynie argued the case for a heightened police presence on preventive grounds: "It is easier to preserve the tranquillity which Parisians currently enjoy than to restore it once it has been disturbed." Police chiefs through the ages would say "amen" to that. There was also the police force of the Lieutenant of the Short Robe (the "short" robe indicating that the Lieutenant, though he had judicial functions, was primarily a man of the sword) which acted as a kind of flying squad against violent crime in the city limits. The Provost of the Ile de France commanded a military force that patrolled the suburbs and the surrounding countryside. There also existed a body of special agents called "exempts," created by Cardinal Mazarin, which was available to assist more senior police officials in investigations and in secret police work. It was an exempt operating for La Reynie, one Desgrez, who disguised himself as a cleric to pursue the Marquise de Brinvilliers, wanted for poisoning her husband and her two brothers, who had fled beyond the frontier. Desgrez charmed her into returning, whereupon she was tried and decapitated.

And, very importantly, there were the ancestors of the commissaires of police of modern times, the *commissaires-enquêteurs au Châtelet,* police officials of magisterial status, who were locally responsible for law and order in each of the sixteen *quartiers,* administrative districts or wards, into which Paris was then divided. They each had a staff of *sergents* (the word comes from the Latin *serviens* and here means a public official, not a sergeant in the military sense) to enforce their orders and, like the other police functionaries mentioned above, they were required to obey the orders of the Lieutenant of Police. The commissaires' office was already ancient, dating from the beginning of the fourteenth century. The inclusion of the word "Châtelet" in their title indicates their connection with the royal courts of justice that sat in the venerable fortress of that name. The Lieutenant of Police, in addition to his official headquarters in the rue Neuve des Capucines, had two rooms allocated to him in the Châtelet, in his capacity as a judge.

La Reynie made a determined attack on the city's crime. Much of this was harbored and fostered in a notorious "no-go" area of central Paris, the Cour des Miracles, the "Court of Miracles," the name of which was derived from reputed cures of infirmities in days gone by and which now had become the riotous and dangerous lair of criminals, beggars, fugitives, and drop-outs. La Reynie mounted his attack on this rats' castle in 1668. The classic description of the operation is given by Horace Raisson in his history of the Paris police:

> La Reynie resolved to go to the Cour des Miracles himself and have done at a single stroke with the place and its fearsome denizens. Preceded by a squadron of sappers of the Swiss Regiment, 150 men of the Watch, a half-squadron of soldiers of the *Maréchaussée,* a com-

missaire and some exempts, the Lieutenant of Police appeared at dawn at the portals of the Cour des Miracles. At the sight of the soldiers the hell-hole's entire population, women, ancients, men, children, began to raise a horrible row: in an instant, sharpened spits, iron-capped sticks, old daggers, blunderbusses and muskets were raised above dishevelled, emaciated, sinister faces on which debauchery, drink and fury were written in lines of bile and dirt. The soldiers, little prepared to fight in such a place and against such adversaries, hesitated to advance and were getting ready to use their arms against the threatening rabble.

"No firing!" cried La Reynie in a voice of thunder, coming to the front rank and imposing silence upon the whole furious mob by his gesture and mien. "I could have you taken and thrown into prison or the galleys: I would rather pardon, for perhaps there are more unlucky people here than guilty ones. Listen to me and be thankful. I am going to have three breaches made in your walls. You will escape freely through the openings. The last twelve left behind will pay for all: six will be hanged and the other six will go the galleys for twenty years."

Terror and dread now froze and reduced to dejection the crowd so menacing a moment before. The sappers were soon at work and three large breaches were made in the mud and wattle walls of the sorry den. La Reynie then had the sappers fall back upon the body of troops who had protected them while they were at work and, in a terrifying, emphatic voice, he cried, "All be off, and woe betide the last twelve!"

It must have been a weird sight, that multitude rushing to the openings the quicker to get away. Each must have recovered some lost sense or missing limb: the blind, sight; the paralytic, agility; the lame, legs, to escape being of the fated dozen and flee from the Minotaur threatening them. In 20 minutes the Cour des Miracles had lost its entire population and when an ingenuous officer of the Watch came to inform La Reynie in a nonplussed manner that he had not been able to catch a single one of the wretches, the Lieutenant of Police replied, "So much the better, Monsieur, and to ensure that they will not return in future, burn the huts, pull down the walls, let there be nothing to see but empty space, and may the last trace of the barbarism of a former age vanish with the Cour des Miracles!"

La Reynie's clemency was to bring certain dividends for the police: some of the former residents of the Cour des Miracles became useful informers.

Louis XIV was credited by Voltaire with the repression of the fashionable evil of duelling, though history records that members of the nobility were not to be denied their age-old resort to the field of honor. La Reynie's assiduous severity in enforcing the law, however, greatly diminished the practice and he also went far in disarming the population by stern action against those not entitled to bear arms.

The Lieutenant of Police, whose title was changed in 1674 to Lieutenant-General of Police, in addition to his regular duties as a criminal judge, was sometimes required by the king to concern himself with matters gravely affecting the well-being of France and the aureole of glory with which Louis XIV always aspired to surround himself. Of such matters, the complex criminal case known as the Affair of the Poisons was surely the most troublesome. It began in 1679 and was discontinued by order of the king in 1682. La Reynie was appointed president and rapporteur of the judicial commission that heard it.

This is not the place to retell the sinister and sorry tale of how people in high society lost all sense of reality and honor and became involved with self-styled sorcerers, quacks, renegade clerics, and poisoners: suffice it to say that even the king's mistress was implicated and the regime was tainted with scandal. Great industry, acute perception, and deep analysis were demanded of La Reynie and no doubt what he had to do caused him endless anxiety and, perhaps, some problems of conscience as a jurist, but the king was the law and La Reynie's loyalty to the throne always had the first claim on him.

The hearings went on at two levels, one regular, one secret. Over three hundred warrants of arrest were issued, thirty-four death sentences were carried out, many were exiled, many more administratively imprisoned in fortresses for the rest of their lives. The full record of the proceedings was known only to the king, the ministers Colbert and Louvois, and La Reynie. The two ministers died, but it was not until after the death of La Reynie that the king had the record burned in his own presence: the Lieutenant-General of Police had enjoyed not only his sovereign's confidence but also his respect.

The outcome of the Affair of the Poisons demonstrates what may become of the rule of law under an autocratic regime. Louis

19

XIV genuinely loved the law, instituted legal reforms, gladly employed grave jurists to serve him; but when the shadow of crime fell upon his own fame he abrogated the judicial procedure and wound up the whole business by executive action.

It would be unfair to overemphasize the repressive aspects of La Reynie's attack on crime. His great contribution to the preventive science of police must not be overlooked. The priority he gave to maintaining a strong patrol presence, his measures for lighting and hygiene, his monumental edict on the control of prostitution which remained in force until 1946, his attempt to find a practical solution to the problem of homeless children by building a foundling hospital, all bear witness to what he achieved in the sphere of urban police science.

The later years of his tenure of office were darkened by the consequences of the king's Revocation of the Edict of Nantes in 1685, which ended the toleration of Protestantism in France for many years to come. The Lieutenant-General of Police was specially commissioned to enforce the measure, which caused a quarter of a million of France's most productive citizens to go into exile (with great benefit to the countries where they settled). La Reynie carried out his orders with loyal sternness, while sometimes counseling moderation in the application of the law.

Grain shortages in 1692 and 1693 made bread scarce and expensive. La Reynie found that his statutory charge to see that Paris had sufficient food at fair prices was a heavy one. The working population's resentment and fury when the staple article of their diet became hard to get led to riots, and the bakers had to be given police protection. The Lieutenant-General and his commissaires found themselves in the grain business as they strove to stimulate the flow of supplies from the rural areas and to reduce the prices of grain and flour.

Among the multifarious duties of the office was the censorship of the press, which La Reynie seems to have exercised diligently but with an understanding in advance of the spirit of the age. A cultured and responsible censor, he caused Molière to make tactful changes in the texts of his plays but made handsome amends to literature by preserving intact for posterity the great dramatist's original manuscripts.

La Reynie probably held his high office too long, as did Sir

Richard Mayne in London in the nineteenth century and John Edgar Hoover in Washington, D.C., in the twentieth. La Reynie was over seventy and his standing was irksome to less able but more influential people around the king. In 1697 he resigned his post, a man of integrity and dedication, disinterested, unassuming. He had even earned the respect of that waspish memorialist of the age, the Duc de Saint-Simon, who expressed surprise that La Reynie took pains to do as little harm as possible when he might have done so much. Saint-Simon concluded: "a man of honour and a great and upright judge."

To the police historian La Reynie will always stand as a great pioneer in the art and science of policing the big city.

The Eighteenth Century

PROVINCIAL CITIES

The success of his police reforms in Paris, together with the irresistible attraction of raising money by selling official posts (during the Ancien Regime all public office was venal: La Reynie, for instance, bought his police charge in 1667 for 150,000 *livres*), encouraged Louis XIV to extend them to the rest of the kingdom. An edict in 1699 ordained that in each of the larger cities there should be a Lieutenant-General of Police who would perform there the principal functions that the Lieutenant-General of Police performed in Paris. These provincial police chiefs would be bound by the latter's general ordinances and he was recognized as having some degree of jurisdiction at the national level. Another Edict of the same year instituted in the larger cities commissaires who would have functions similar to those of the *commissaires enquêteurs au Châtelet*.

The king's intention was to cut through the tangle of local jurisdictions and impose a uniform standard of urban policing throughout France. This threatened a considerable encroachment upon the independence of the municipalities. Since the Middle Ages they had maintained their own forces to preserve order and repress wrongdoers within their walls. Their reaction to the king's measures was to take advantage of the new police offices being up for sale: they simply bought their way into the system.

In Marseille the mayor, four deputy mayors, and an assessor acquired a collective charge, "all six being jointly and severally Lieutenants-General of Police." "City Hall" usually purchased the new offices. In Lyon the city fathers paid 180,000 *livres* for the posts of a Lieutenant-General, a prosecutor, a clerk, ten commissaires, and six process servers. Sometimes the posts were bought by the courts, or by royal provosts, even by ecclesiastical officials.

The municipalities, in fact, were in control of their own police arrangements, but royal intervention was always possible. Until 1789 the Intendant of Justice, Police, and Finance had the last word on police matters and could requisition civil and military forces in his province.

THE *MARÉCHAUSSÉE*

Meanwhile, in the less populated areas, in the villages and countryside, along the roads, France's soldier-police were maintaining their hard-faced vigil. The *maréchaussée,* the military police from which the Gendarmerie Nationale is directly descended, may be traced, perhaps with a little imagination, to the élite warriors, the *gens d'armes,* the "men-at-arms" who formed the king's bodyguard in battle. It was they who stood round the royal standard with Saint-Louis, the Crusader-King, in the wars in the Holy Land, and protected his royal successors in the great fights with the English during the Hundred Years War. The "bodyguard" function is still performed today: the Republican Guard of the Gendarmerie Nationale stands outside the front door of the president of France.

A second function fell to the *maréchaussée:* the policing of the royal armies. The provost function is still one of the important duties of the Gendarmerie Nationale. The name *maréchaussée* is derived from the military police in medieval times having been under the Marshals (*Maréchaux*) of France, commanders of the royal armies. At the outset a single provost answered to them but as the numbers and missions of the army multiplied, it became necessary to have several provosts, operating under a provost-general. A Constable (military commander-in-chief) of France, Arthur III of Brittany, brought the military police up to substantial numbers in 1439, when fifteen mounted companies were formed. In 1448, infantry was added to the provost troops.

The movement of formations of soldiers about the country meant that the provosts, their staffs, and troops had to lead an itinerant life, dealing out summary justice and maintaining good order and discipline wherever camps were pitched or troops moved into barracks or billets. The provosts' jurisdiction had originally been confined to the army but the volume of crime in Renaissance France, with which the civil authorities could not cope outside the cities, led to an extension of the scope of the *maréchaussée;* this proved to be the third major aspect of their evolution.

King Francis I, by a declaration in 1536, gave the military police powers to deal with all crime committed on the roads. This marks the development from a purely military status to the dual status of the Gendarmerie today. The provosts, who were judges as well as military officers, now had jurisdiction over civilians as well as soldiers, a jurisdiction that was much extended as time went on.

While the municipal authorities of the cities had means to suffice for the day-to-day police service, they could not usually cope with any collective violence on a large scale. In such cases, the *maréchaussée* were expected to lend their aid. This foreshadows the modern role of the Gendarmerie Mobile.

The *maréchaussée* had long been regarded as a source of general intelligence by the royal government. Francis I, to whom his soldier-police were "the arm that bears up my sceptre," instructed the provosts on their journeys to use their eyes and ears and inform him of any abuses. Eighteenth-century orders to the provosts were "to keep the Intendant informed of all matters of interest to police and administration in their area and to be on trusting and cordial terms with the Mayors." The widespread presence of the small units of the military police, always among the people, was a great intelligence resource during the Ancien Regime. It still is.

Until 1720 the *maréchaussée* had been a somewhat miscellaneous body, operating on a provincial or local basis, with much variety in quality and pay. There had been room in its heterogeneous organization for a company to be allocated to Joan of Arc for her bodyguard and for one to be under the personal command of Cardinal Mazarin (room, too, for Athos, Porthos, Aramis, and d'Artagnan). The usual operational method had been the cavalry sweep in response to outbreaks; this would now give way to a more static and preventive system.

The Ordinance of 1720, the work of Charles Leblanc, then Minister of War, marks the further evolution of the *maréchaussée* into a national as opposed to a provincial organization. The form of the territorial company was now prescribed: provost in command, with court staff and legal officers for judicial purposes, lieutenants, noncommissioned officers, and men for policing. The police element was divided, overall, into 565 five-man squads (*brigades*), stationed at ten- or twelve-mile intervals along the main roads, each squad having its own sector to patrol. The companies were grouped into inspectoral districts for supervision and higher command. The network thus formed in 1720 is the basic network of the Departmental Gendarmerie today.

Most important of the subsequent measures with respect to the *maréchaussée* that were taken during what remained of the Ancien Regime was Louis XVI's Ordinance of 1778, which brought the corps into line with the rest of the army. The *maréchaussée* was given precedence after the Gendarmerie of the Royal Household. The basic unit was reduced to three men under a noncommissioned officer. The patrol routine was laid down, the duties specified. Even the form of the barracks, the *hôtel de la maréchaussée,* was prescribed. At this time the corps comprised thirty-three companies, in six divisions under inspectors-general.

Thus, in the last half-century of the Ancien Regime, the hundreds of years of development of France's military police had culminated in an organizational completeness that the stormy future would modify but which is still radically the same.

PARIS

Thirteen Lieutenants-General of Police followed La Reynie between 1697 and 1789. Like him, they had begun their careers as lawyers and had bought into the body of royal legal officials called *maîtres des requêtes,* whose posts were of magisterial status and afforded a great variety of both legal and administrative experience. Their passage through their high office, however briefly noted, serves to illustrate its many facets and hazards, the importance of their individual characters, and the comprehensive nature of the Ancien Regime's concept of police.

Marc-René Levoyer de Paulmy, Marquis d'Argenson, succeeded La Reynie with great distinction, holding the top police post for twenty-one years. Perhaps his greatest charactistic was his vitality, which enabled him to turn night into day and enjoy work and leisure with equal appetite. Ugly as Satan, he had much of Satan's charm—Shakespeare says "The Prince of Darkness is a gentleman", but if the marquis was not on the side of the angels, he was very much on the side of law and order.

A great administrator, he was able to tackle a multiplicity of problems with rare presence of mind. He developed the political intelligence side of his work, making systematic use of informers. Realizing the need for more investigative agents on the ground, he was instrumental in the creation in 1708 of forty (later reduced to twenty) posts for inspectors, whom he allocated as necessary to the commissaires to assist them in detecting breaches of the police regulations, always keeping two at his own disposal. Some of his successors found rather odd jobs for them, including the writing of pornographic reports for the diversion of the Court.

It fell to d'Argenson, as it had to La Reynie, to enforce the royal policy in matters of religion: to censor the work of the liberal Archbishop Fénelon and to shut down the austere but unorthodox Convent of Port-Royal.

Paris's police map was changed by d'Argenson, when the sixteen *quartiers* in 1702 became twenty, with a corresponding increase in the number of commissaires.

He enjoyed the respect of the ordinary people of Paris by reason of the courage he showed in leading his men from the front at outbreaks of fire, on one occasion staying on his feet for twenty hours on end, and also of his readiness to face angry mobs and open up dialogue with them. He was always attentive, too, to the lighting and cleaning of the streets. It is a mark of his popular authority that he survived in office after the dire food shortages of 1709, when he showed the utmost determination and resourcefulness in maintaining public order. D'Argenson pioneered the idea of a number of fixed police stations (later extended by his son) where people could be sure of finding help.

His friend the writer Fontenelle divined the secret, perhaps, of his police success: "to ignore what it is better to ignore than to punish, and to punish only rarely and usefully."

The monarchy and Paris were lucky that in its first half-century the Lieutenancy of Police had such superior and unsparing public servants. Voltaire wrote of d'Argenson:

> *Vigilant genius,*
> *Generous successor to the prudent La Reynie,*
> *To whom Paris owes everything.*

Very few of their successors were to approach them in quality.

Machault d'Arnouville lasted only two years, unable to ride out the scandal of a marshal of France being attacked in his coach by bandits in Paris. Taschereau de Baudry made his name by harsh ordinances against bearing arms and soldiers out at night without leave; he enjoined householders to lock their doors early in the hours of darkness; he restricted the movement of domestic servants without certificates from their employers. He forbade anyone to leave the kingdom without a passport, on pain of death. His prohibitive view of his functions was no doubt the reason for his tenure, too, only lasting two years. D'Argenson's son, Pierre-Marc Levoyer de Paulmy had two brief periods as Lieutenant-General before being appointed Minister of War. He showed his father's courage in fighting fires and the Paris fire service was developed in his time (1722–1724), with two hundred firemen and twenty-five fire stations. The Paris fire service, incidentally, is still under the administration of the Prefect of Police.

Ravot d'Ombreval must be remembered for his creation of the Bourse, the Paris Stock Exchange. He applied himself to the regulation of public vehicles and street nuisances, but a rise in the price of bread turned the people against him and in 1725 he had to go.

René Hérault had some fourteen years of undistinguished office. His vision was limited by his religious convictions: he was addicted to the persecution of unorthodoxy and of freemasonry. He nevertheless contributed to Parisian well-being by having the names of the streets placarded at intersections. He also closed down the last of the Cours des Miracles at Saint-Médard. Someone pinned up an epigram:

By the King's order, God must not
Perform his miracles on this spot.

His son-in-law, Feydeau de Marville, paved four districts of the city and built the rue Feydeau. He established regular contact with the king but displeased the royal mistress, Madame de Pompadour, which brought about his downfall.

One of her protegés replaced him, Nicolas-René Berryer, who held office from 1747 to 1757. He was as assiduous in informing his patroness as his predecessor had been in informing the king, which may account for the length of his tenure. A police innovation in his time was the creation of an office called the *Bureau de Sûreté* (Security Office) where people could come to report thefts; the officials there had to accept the information without charging the fees usually exacted by the commissaires for this service. Lenoir, one of the best of his successors, regarded Berryer as the principal builder of the system of domestic espionage, for which he contrived to obtain extraordinary financing. Berryer made indiscriminate war on vagabonds and beggars, his men sometimes arresting the wrong people. The people came to have a fierce animosity against him. The younger d'Argenson, one of his predecessors, wrote in his diary for May 29, 1750: "Monsieur Berryer is above all hated by the people, whom he has treated brutally, having no common touch of any kind. He is a little pedant, overbearing and self-sufficient. The populace talk of nothing but killing him." But he had harassed the freemasons (whose lodges nevertheless continued to increase in number) and provided Madame de Pompadour with a chronicle of activity in the brothels, and the king made him Minister of Justice.

Madame de Pompadour was able to place another of her protegés to succeed him. Bertin de Bellisle is remembered for causing the Veterinary School to be built at Alfort and he issued useful regulations for public hygiene. The king made him Minister of Finance.

Antoine-Raymond-Jean-Gualbert de Sartines held the Lieutenancy-General of Police from 1759 to 1774. He was one of the great police myth-makers. He worshipped at the shrine of Intelligence, multiplying his sources of information, and succeeded in putting over the idea that his police were omniscient and omnipresent. Assuredly, he was more than capable in manipulating the systems of information that Berryer had built, the value of intelligence depending on the quality of the persons who receive it, but when he complacently told King Louis XV that when three people were talking in the street, one of them was undoubtedly his, one may take leave to wonder whether over half a million people in one city contained such a large proportion of informers. The modern *reductio ad absurdum* of this boast is that when three people are talking politics in Moscow, two are members of the KGB and the third is a lunatic.

Myth-maker as he was, de Sartines was also a highly efficient police administrator. He built up the fire and river rescue services and vastly improved the street lighting by converting it from candle lanterns to oil lamps. The municipal police work was excellently performed, with much attention to public hygiene, drains, and street cleaning. He encouraged technical education, founding a free School of Design for craftsmen and began the construction of the Halle aux Blés, the Corn Market.

Most important of all, he maintained a high level of public tranquillity in the capital. He was exceptionally able in dealing with crowds and once, when there was a rowdy demonstration on the Place Maubert, de Sartines, having as usual turned up promptly at the scene of trouble, gave some instructions to one of the young officers of his mounted force. The officer rode forward, took off his hat, and said, "We come in the King's name, but we only have orders to fire on the mob. I ask respectable people to withdraw." Perhaps they *were* respectable people, or perhaps their vanity was touched, but in any event they dispersed.

De Sartines acquired an international reputation for his police insight and knowledge; the Empress Maria Theresa of Austria, even the Pope, consulted him. He anticipated Napoleon's police minister, Fouché by operating a discreet foreign-intelligence system. He loved the dramatic aspects of his role. It was said that he would not receive a duke in the same wig in which he would receive a marquis, and while he was engaged in endless work of genuine value to the community, he still found time to divert the

Court with a "confidential" bulletin of scandal. When Louis XVI succeeded to the throne, dazzled, he invited the prestigious master of the police to become his First Minister. De Sartines, the realist, knowing his own limitations, contented himself with the post of Minister of Marine.

He had a worthy successor in Jean Lenoir, whose first tenure of the police magistracy was rudely curtailed by bread rioting, when he was let down by Marshal Biron's refusal to bring troops to the aid of the civil power. Briefly replaced by Joseph Albert, he was restored to office for the period 1776 to 1785, years of dedicated and fruitful administration. He occupied himself with the detail of municipal services—street lamps, street cleaning, hygiene in bars and dairies; he had first-aid equipment placed in every commissaire's office; he founded a bakery school, and schools for children of the poor. He began the vast task of clearing of the Innocents Cemetery, where over a million and a half cadavers were threatening to pollute the city's water supply. His lasting monument is France's system of state pawn shops, the Crédit Municipal of today, which he founded to enable people to borrow money at better rates than the moneylenders offered.

Thiroux de Crosne, who followed Lenoir, was to be the last Lieutenant-General of Police. He completed the clearance of the Innocents Cemetery and began public works to employ the poor. But the great storm was gathering and this mild, good man, with his highly creditable background of public administration, had neither the perspicacity nor the resources to weather it.

At the End of an Era

When an attempt is made to evaluate the stewardship of the Lieutenants-General of Police from 1667 to 1789, the balance sheet has impressive entries on both the credit and the debit sides.

The rehabilitation of public safety and urban order had been highly successful: Paris in the eighteenth century was very much safer for the ordinary citizen than was London or Rome. The police presence, the fire service, public hygiene, all under a single direction, were very much superior to anything London could show. The relief of the poor, the care of the sick, the educational and training facilities, under that same direction, again were superior, reflecting enlightenment and humanity. The streets and public buildings of Paris bear enduring witness to the civic spirit of the Lieutenants-General. Their continuous preoccupation with the city's economy—its food supply, its prices, its markets—surely saved the people from greater hardship and exploitation than might have been their lot under unfettered private enterprise.

The policing of Paris, however, was performed under the authority of an autocratic monarch who, while he often excelled in the benefits he conferred upon his subjects, also encroached on their freedom. During the eighteenth century French political thinkers found much virtue in the constitutional order in England and in the principles of the American Revolution. It became intolerable to the new liberalism to contemplate a king above the law, able to have arbitrary arrests made and to imprison people, sometimes for life, without trial. The *lettre de cachet* (letter with seal), a warrant under the royal seal for arrest and detention, was particularly anathematized by critics of the regime, though documents extensively analyzed in the twentieth century revealed little evidence that this device had been tyrannically used against the people at large. It was normally used to keep the nobility in order, to prevent families being discredited by wicked or scandalous behavior. Also, when the cumbrous processes of law might fail to do justice, discretionary action by the king could resolve a case in the light of common sense. The *lettre de cachet,* nevertheless, understandably came to symbolize the king's superiority to the law and the officers who served it were criticized in the same terms as their royal master.

The police's responsibility for censorship and their control of printing and the distribution of publications inevitably blackened their character at a time when discussion had become all the rage. The proliferation of masonic lodges, which police persecution had apparently caused to thrive, provided an influential forum for criticism of the regime. The ruthless imposition of religious orthodoxy in years not long gone by, in which the police had to play a highly visible part, was a further instance to the critics' minds of the king's determination to abolish freedom of thought. As "thought-police," however, the Lieutenants-General must be considered abysmal failures.

Individual liberty was also encroached upon by the extraordinary degree of surveillance exercised by the police. An exasperated Briton, visiting France in the early 1780s, wrote that "they attend to the very meals you eat and the *Lieutenant of the Police* is as well informed of the meat you have eaten, as the *Traiteur* who dressed it." Throughout the eighteenth century the French had been uncomfortably conscious of domestic espionage by the authorities, the all-pervasive presence of spies at all levels making secret and uncontrolled reports on everyone and everything. D'Argenson, asked by Louis XIV where he recruited his secret agents, is reputed to have replied, "In all classes, Sire, but particularly among dukes and lackeys." Even the beneficent Lenoir is said to have had a quarter of the maids and lackeys in Paris in his pay and Thiroux de Crosne, well-meaning to a fault, nevertheless pleaded for more money to pay informers. Long before the Ancien Regime came to an end, the French were thoroughly familiar with the practice of compiling secret dossiers on individuals who had committed no crime but had "come to the notice of the authorities." Another reprehended surveillance technique was "the black cabinet" business of opening, reading, and resealing letters in transit. The brothel, as always, was a source of criminal intelligence, and could also provide a "hold" on someone, or be the source of scabrous writings to amuse the royal circle. The police tolerated brothels for a variety of reasons, but they drew a large income from gambling houses, money that went into their secret funds.

The account, as between police and citizen, is hard to balance. The Revolution would seek to redress that balance, earnestly, ardently, violently.

CHAPTER 3

The Revolution

July 1789

The causes of the Revolution that began in 1789 were involute, social, economic, political, intellectual. The richest and most populous country in Europe was bankrupt. The king, Louis XVI, with the best intentions, summoned the States-General, the assembly of the Three Estates of the Realm, Clergy, Nobility, and Commons. Their last meeting had been in 1614. Now they met at Versailles on May 4, 1789. Their agenda, whether they knew it or not, was the future of France.

The question of where, or whether, the police were at fault in the years that preceded the coming of the Revolution is one which clearly has to be asked. How far it can be answered is less clear.

The movement of public opinion was certainly a matter for police concern. In the impossible task of suppressing all discussion, all political and philosophical groups criticizing the existing order and propounding reform, the police, as mentioned above, can only be said to have failed. In recording this conclusion one can only ask who now would have wished them to succeed? Their failure to chart the current of public opinion and to present it to the king and his ministers must nevertheless be held against them.

The agricultural crisis of 1788 was the worst for over a century, the winter bringing disastrous shortages of food and widespread unemployment. France's was preponderantly an agrarian economy, with four-fifths of the population working on the land. The spring of 1789 found Paris thronged with workless, homeless people, refugees from the stricken countryside, vainly seeking employment in the city. The classic responsibility of the Lieutenant-General of Police for seeing that the capital was adequately provisioned was certainly not carried out, but, in the wholly exceptional circumstances, it is only fair to wonder if it could have been.

In their handling of the public turbulence of those months, there may be firmer grounds for finding fault with the police. The Lieutenant-General's forces showed little expertise, vacillating between weak reaction and excessive use of force. Crowd control was poor and failed to prevent such incidents as the mob killings of two manufacturers, Reveillon and Hanriot, who had made silly remarks in public about the cost of living and the improvidence of the poor. Police intelligence completely failed to gauge the temper of the populace; no dispositions seem to have been made to prepare for the contingency of street riots. Looting and the breaking open of prisons occurred, with large-scale violence on July 12, 1789.

The middle classes, fearful of a take-over by the wilder elements, took desperate steps to procure arms; a dreadful rumor of German mercenaries coming in to massacre the citizens ran through Paris like wildfire. The Hôtel de Ville, Paris's City Hall, yielded its store of weapons. The next day cannon and a great quantity of muskets were seized from the Invalides, the monumental veterans' hospital built by Louis XIV. By now the bourgeois had been joined by the perennial recruits to riot situations, the idle, mischievous, and criminal members of the populace. The outbreaks in Paris were in large part reactions to the news at national level that filtered in from Versailles.

On July 14, 1789, the Bastille, a royal fortress within the city walls, was attacked by disaffected soldiers of the French Guards and by the mob. The governor, prevented by the garrison from blowing up the powder magazine, surrendered. Promised safe conduct, he was butchered by the mob while being taken under guard to the Hôtel de Ville.

In the larger context of the total force available to the authorities to suppress the rising, the role and responsibility of the Lieutenant-General of Police are much diminished. The king at Versailles had six thousand troops under Marshal de Broglie, and Paris was encircled by ten thousand troops, mostly of Swiss and German regiments, under Baron de Besenval. Besenval, dubious of whether his men would fire on the people, never brought them to a confrontation. The traditional last resort in cases of dire civil disorder, the Army, had failed. Paris was no longer under royal control.

Reform

The Declaration of Rights of August 26, 1789, spoke out against the police evils of the Ancien Regime. There was to be individual liberty and freedom of opinion; no man was to be accused, arrested, or imprisoned except by due process of law; there was to be freedom of speech, liberty of the press, religious toleration.

For over two years after the classic date of its commencement, July 14, 1789, the Revolution proceeded with the king and his ministers in theory and in some respects in practice at the head of affairs.

The police system of the Ancien Regime was largely dismantled. The abolition of the venality, the purchase and sale, of public office on August 4, 1789, swept away the Lieutenancy-General of Police, the *commissaires-enquêteurs au Châtelet* and the inspectors of police. Thiroux de Crosne had handed over all his functions on July 16th to Bailly, mayor of a newly civic Paris. Bailly established himself in de Crosne's former headquarters as head of a Provisional Committee of Police, Security, and Tranquillity, which received royal approval on August 5th. A particularly horrible killing by the mob of a baker under arrest on a charge of hoarding caused the Minister of Justice to require the Paris Municipal Council to seek out the perpetrators. The council promptly formed a Committee of Investigation, appointed from its own members, to receive denunciations and depositions regarding plots and conspiracies, to secure and interrogate persons denounced and to assemble proofs to build up cases.

The *commissaires-enquêteurs au Châtelet* were replaced in May 1790 by a commissaire of police for each of the forty-eight sections that had replaced the former *quartiers*. The commissaires of police were locally elected for two years, each of them being associated with and supervised by sixteen "section commissaires." Also locally elected were the commissaires' secretaries and clerks. In September 1791, the Ancien Regime's inspectors of police were replaced by twenty-four *officiers de paix* (peace officers), appointed by the Municipal Council. In the same month the office of commissaire of police was instituted in the urban centers of the provinces, elected, as in Paris, and very dependent on the local municipality. The legislature repeatedly urged the importance of having the commissaires of police in place. Instead of the judicial wig and long robe worn by the Ancien Regime's commissaires, the commissaire of police was distinguished by a tricolour knot on the left shoulder, ancestor of the tricolour sash worn by the commissaire of police today.

One of the great police institutions of the Ancien Regime did not perish amid the flood of innovation. The *maréchaussée,* after a brief suspension—they had remained at their posts with true military nonchalance—were reconstituted with effect from February 15, 1791, under the name they bear today, the Gendarmerie Nationale. The strength was fixed at 7,455 gendarmes. The judicial function of the provosts and the office of provost were abolished. Their function was to remain as before: the policing of the countryside, though if legally called upon, they could operate within city limits. The Revolution held to the principle that military force could only be used at the request of the civil power.

The most visible of the revolutionary police forces was the National Guard, first commanded by the Marquis de La Fayette, French hero of the War of American Independence. Created on July 14, 1789, recognized by a decree of 1790, the National Guard had a battalion in each of Paris's forty-eight sections by August 1792.

It was expected—vainly—that these committees, elected police officials and ad hoc soldiers would suffice to maintain order in a capital city in which revolutionary fury and criminal violence were fermenting with ever-increasing intensity while prostitution and gambling enjoyed a new license. The abolition of the institutions of justice and police to which people had been accustomed for so long encouraged malefactors all over France to believe that they could now take the offensive with impunity. For many years to come banditry would flourish. The steady, systematic work and the day-to-day surveillance of a police machine long adapted to its purpose could not be replaced by the idealistic and experimental devices of the new age.

The last days of the National Assembly in Versailles saw the Paris prison massacres of September 1792, when 1,300 people were killed after travesties of trials. France was now at war and war fever added its own sickness to the hectic confusion of the time.

On September 21, 1792, the National Convention, successor to the National Assembly, held its first session and abolished the monarchy. Louis XVI's trial by the Convention began on December 10th. He was guillotined on January 21, 1793.

Terror

Beset by enemies at home and abroad, at war with Britain and the monarchies of Europe, the Revolution's interior defense was terror.

The ministries of the late king's government were replaced by committees formed from the membership of the National Convention. The Committee of General Security, under Marc Vadier, was established in September 1792. A lawyer by profession, Vadier was to be the political police chief of the Terror, "the old inquisitor," as many called him. He sat beside the Public Prosecutor at the trial by the Convention of Marie-Antoinette (she was guillotined in 1794) and made frequent visits to the Revolutionary Tribunal to ensure that due severity prevailed. His committee had police jurisdiction on a national scale, arresting all and sundry on suspicion of disaffection or crime.

The Committee of Public Safety, at first under Danton, then under Robespierre, was formed in April 1793, and became the ruling organ of the Republic. As such, it frequently and blatantly encroached upon Vadier's sphere. Danton and Robespierre were statesmen, leaders, and guardians of the revolutionary spirit; Vadier was a political police chief. As an example of encroachment, it may be noted that the Committee of Public Safety set up a Central Police Bureau. It also re-created the "black cabinet" of the Ancien Regime, intercepting letters in course of post.

The Reign of Terror, designed to hold the Republic together and to dragoon the divided nation into unity, began with the passing of the Law of Suspects by the National Convention on September 17, 1793. This, with the vagueness characteristic of revolutionary legislation, gave the Committee of Public Safety the right to arrest anyone suspected to be lacking in revolutionary orthodoxy. Aristocrats, members of opposition groups in the Convention, revolutionaries who had not kept up to the mark—among them Danton, Camille Desmoulins, who had first called for the assault on the Bastille in 1789, and Bailly, first mayor of Paris—were brought before the Revolutionary Tribunal and sent to the scaffold. The executioners worked hard every day to carry out the sentences demanded by Fouquier-Tinville, the Public Prosecutor.

These were perilous days for the French Republic. Externally at war, within its own borders the new state had to fight not only disorder and dissension but also the determination of certain parts of France to reject the Revolution and go their own way. The National Convention, lacking high-level administrators and police chiefs outside Paris, began to send out its own members, "Representatives on Mission," to enforce its policies in the provinces.

They brought the Terror to the cities of France. Citizen-Representative Joseph Le Bon had 150 prominent citizens guillotined in Cambrai and 400 more in Arras. Marseille, Toulon, Bordeaux, the Army of the Rhine, all felt the heavy and implacable rage of the plenipotentiaries of the Committee of Public Safety. The Vendée, comprising the former provinces of Brittany, Poitou, and Anjou, revolted in 1793, standing up against the Convention's anti-Catholic measures and affirming the cause of royalism. A full-scale war, with many thousands of dead, had to be waged against the peasants by the soldiers of the Republic before the region was subjugated. Citizen-Representative J.B. Carrier, in the wake of the army, came to stamp out what remained of the rebellion, allowing thousands of people to be drowned in the city of Nantes.

When Lyon, second city of France, rebelled and overthrew the revolutionary regime there, once the Republic's troops, after a two-month siege, had retaken it, the Committee of Public Safety despatched representatives to deal out revolutionary justice. Collot d'Herbois and Joseph Fouché did not shrink from carrying out their mandate. Under their surveillance, the Revolutionary Tribunal sentenced 1,667 people to death. This was too great a task for the overworked guillotine so the citizen-representatives had the executions carried out by cannon fire. They also demolished large areas of the city, which thus lost 1,600 houses.

The draconian measures of the Committee of Public Safety saved the Republic from breaking up, forcing unity at home while their armies in the field triumphed against France's enemies. But in the atmosphere of governmental terrorism, targeted against the Revolution's political foes, ordinary police work was neglected and the country was ravaged by crime and vice.

Reaction

Once the republican armies began to get the upper hand in their struggle with the European monarchs, the justification of the Terror declined and there was a feeling that too much blood had been shed, especially in the provinces. Robespierre began to move against those who had been the agents of the Committee of Public Safety's terrorist policies: among them was Joseph Fouché, whom Robespierre declared he was determined to destroy.

A coalition of those who were threatened, probably mastized behind the scenes by Fouché, who was lying low, attacked Robespierre in the National Convention on July 27, 1794 (9th Thermidor, in the republican calendar). He was arrested, brought to trial, and guillotined with twenty of his supporters the following day. Fouquier-Tinville, the Public Prosecutor of the Terror, was indicted the following month and also found his way to the scaffold. Saint-Just, grand theorist of the militant Revolution, had died with Robespierre.

The events of Thermidor, portentous as they were, did nothing to improve the wretched state of day-to-day policing. The National Convention cast about for measures to allay the public's dissatisfaction. In 1795 it decided that commissaires of police should no longer be elected but appointed by the Committee of General Security; a few months later it decided that municipalities should make these appointments. A list was drawn up of all the communes which were to have commissariats of police, and it was decreed that Paris, Lyon, Bordeaux, Toulon, and Marseille should each have a Central Police Bureau. The dislocation caused by the breaking up of the Ancien Regime's system was not to be remedied by such paper solutions: common crime flourished and violent political outbreaks continued. The Convention itself was invaded in April 1795 by the armed populace, and reacted by disbanding the Paris gendarmerie and National Guard troops who had failed to protect it. A Legion of General Police, seven thousand hastily recruited men, instituted to replace them, proved even less reliable, indiscipline and disaffection rendering them useless, and had to be abolished in 1796. Another of the Convention's apparently mindless acts was to abolish also the *officiers de paix*.

On October 5, 1795, the Convention was again the subject of armed attack, this time in the form of a royalist rising. A brigadier-general of artillery was sent for to defend the masters of France, which he duly did by bringing up cannon and dispersing the rebel forces with his celebrated "whiff of grapeshot." Napoleon Bonaparte had succeeded in his first police operation.

On the day before its dissolution, which took place on October 26, 1795, the National Convention produced a Police Code which, among its other virtues, gave some valuable definitions:

> The police is instituted to maintain public order and tranquillity, liberty, property, individual security.... The administrative police has as its object the regular maintenance of public order.... Its principal aim is to prevent breaches of the law. It causes the laws, ordinances and regulations of public order to be executed.... The judicial police investigates the felonies, misdemeanors and violations which the administrative police has not been able to prevent, assembles proof of them and delivers the perpetrators to the courts charged to punish them.

Definitions, indeed, of the police task, but the task itself was not being performed.

The National Convention was succeeded by a bicameral legislature comprising the Council of Five Hundred and the Coun-

39

cil of Ancients (250 in number), with an executive of five Directors. The government of the Directory would last just one week longer than four years.

The principal police achievement of the Directory, which genuinely wanted to restore good policing, was the creation of a Ministry of Police, with overall responsibility for national security and order. The Directors explained to the Council of Five Hundred when proposing the new ministry that they were "convinced that it is easier to maintain public tranquillity than to re-establish it once it has been disturbed." Perhaps they had been reading La Reynie's letter to Colbert of over a century before: as the Revolution aged, its leaders tended more and more to look back to the Ancien Regime.

Establishing the ministry proved easier than finding a good minister, but at least a central bureaucratic police institution had been put in place and one of the nine ministers who held office between January 1796 and July 1799 succeeded in catching a dangerous conspirator, the extreme socialist Babeuf, and in reinstituting the *officiers de paix.*

The tenth Minister of General Police of the Directory had previously made a spectacular appearance on the police scene. There was understandable apprehension when he appeared again. The new minister was Joseph Fouché, sanguinary author of the cannonade of Lyon, deadly architect of the destruction of Robespierre.

High Police

Fouché, born in 1759 of a well-to-do family of shipowners near Nantes, had been intended for a maritime career but his health proved too delicate and it was decided that he should study to be a teacher. Educated by the Oratorian Fathers, he spent his youth and young manhood in the cloistered world of the seminary, wearing the habit of the order, being addressed as "Father" by his pupils, but taking no irrevocable vows. The years of mathematics, physics, and logic, the austere and disciplined life of a religious college, the ample time for reflection, all left their enduring mark of composure and serenity on the man who, having achieved the post of prefect and acting head of his academy, decided to leave the world of education for the world of revolutionary politcs.

His lack of ecclesiastical vocation was reflected in his initiation into freemasonry and his marriage. His political aptitude was reflected in his election in 1792 to the National Convention. There he moved rapidly from the waning Right to the waxing Left. He voted for the death of Louis XVI ("in politics," he wrote later, "might atrocity sometimes have its salutary aspect?"), and, as mentioned above, went out as a representative on mission. After Robespierre's death he found it expedient to withdraw for a time into obscurity, whence he was rescued by Barras, one of the five Directors, and given ambassadorial appointments, in Milan and at the Hague. Those who had known the radical revolutionary of the Terror were astonished by the perfect courtesy and easiness of address of the high official of the Directory.

The Ministry of Police was in poor shape when he moved into its headquarters. None of his nine predecessors had had much idea of the purpose and potential of the post. Fouché swiftly took stock, brought his resources under control, and reorganized them. Alive as he was, however, to the need for routine, he never lost sight of the larger issues.

His first preoccupation would always be *la haute police,* high police, the police of politics, the police of the security of the state. He wrote in his memoirs:

> The Crown only succumbed in 1789 through the nullity of the high police, those who were then in charge of it not having been able to penetrate the conspiracies which menaced the royal house. Every government needs as first guarantee of its security a vigilant police, whose chiefs are firm and enlightened. The task of the high police is immense, whether it has to operate within the combinations of a representative government, incompatible with that which is arbitrary and affording factious persons legal weapons for conspiring, or whether it works for the benefit of a government more concentrated, aristocratic, directoral or despotic. The task is all the more difficult in that nothing takes place outwardly: it is in obscurity and mystery that the traces visible only to investigating and penetrating eyes are to be discovered. I found myself in the former case, with the double mission of bringing to light and dissolving legal coalitions and opposition against the established powers, as well as the deep conspiracies of the Royalists and foreign agents.

41

In his high police role, Fouché did not rely upon the written reports of his innumerable agents and informers. Instead, he made himself the most approachable potentate in France, being convinced that it was only by contact with influential people, representing different opinions and schools of thought, different interests and commitments, that he would be able to divine what was really going on in the world. Jacobins, Royalists, middle-of-the-road members of the majority—he saw to it that all felt they had access to the minister and would enjoy his consideration.

The greatest dangers in the interior of France were at the two extremes of the political spectrum. On the one hand there were the revolutionaries who were bent on destroying the middle-class regime that had so exasperatingly emerged from all the hopes and dreams of the Revolution. On the other hand there were the royalists who were bent on restoring the monarchy and with it their own predominance. At this time the former were the more dangerous.

The most virulent of the revolutionary factions were the Jacobins, whose forum was now their clubhouse in the rue du Bac. They had powerful members, including the Minister of War, General Bernadotte, in those days a hard-line partisan of the Left. The Minister of Police, nevertheless, was determined to strike. He saw Bernadotte and gave him warning not to be at the club with effect from tomorrow: "If I find you at the head of it, yours will be off your shoulders. I give you my word for it, and I shall keep it." The soldier realized that he meant what he said and survived to become a Marshal of the Empire and King of Sweden. On August 14, 1799, Fouché, accompanied by a few police officers, presented himself at the club in his official capacity, entered while the inflammatory oratory was at its height, informed the members that the club was now closed, and saw them file confusedly out. He locked the door after them and came away with the keys in his pocket. At about the same time, however, he ordered the deportation of some right-wing property owners and editors and sequestered some royalist property in the Vendée, while paradoxically easing the anti-Royalist regulations. He saw the way forward lay in his being all things to all men.

He was only too well aware that he was serving in a doomed administration. The government of the Directory was adrift on a sea of troubles. The Directors knew it. The solution that occurred to them was to find themselves a successful general—"a head and a sword"—to give the government authority. Various generals were considered. Time was running out, though Fouché had brought them some. The Jacobins and the royalists were plotting the overthrow of the Directory.

At this juncture, General Bonaparte returned from Egypt, where he had abandoned his army in a hopeless situation (he did not mention this) after early victories. Refusing to submit to quarantine, he landed and sped to Paris. The Directors were alarmed. Bonaparte was not on their list of candidate-generals and they asked the Minister of Police whether Bonaparte should be arrested. The minister, who was not surprised by his arrival (Madame Bonaparte was on his secret payroll), said he thought that surveillance was all that was necessary.

Fouché called on the general and gave him his pitiless assessment of the state of the Directory's affairs. Bonaparte was now conspiring busily, as Fouché well knew, but he did not see fit to report this to the Directors. He resolved, though, to make it quite clear what Fouché knew and where Fouché stood. He therefore invited twenty-four members of Bonaparte's conspiracy to dinner and invited Bonaparte to meet them. From that moment, Fouché was Bonaparte's principal source of political intelligence.

At any time in the seven weeks between Bonaparte's landing and the coup d'état that brought him to power, Fouché could have destroyed him. That he did not was because he believed Bonaparte was the man France needed to put her house in order.

So, when the moment came on "18th Brumaire" (November 9, 1799), when Bonaparte and his myrmidons rode out to Saint-Cloud where the two Councils of the Legislature were in session to seize power from them, Fouché secured Paris. The following day Bonaparte was elected First of the Three Consuls to whom the government of France was now entrusted. Fouché was appointed Minister of Police of the Consulate.

CHAPTER 4

Napoleon

Administration

It is understandable that Napoleon Bonaparte should have his primary place in popular recollection as a soldier; during the fifteen years when he was in power, for only fourteen months was France at peace. His forty battles, the triumphs and tragedies of his wars, have overshadowed his even greater political, juridical, and administrative achievements.

The police system was a key part of the Napoleonic state, a state characterized above all by its centralization of power. During the Revolutionary period, when France almost broke apart, the parliamentary government in Paris had moved towards regaining some of the central control which the monarchy, however weakly, had exercised. The National Convention's despatch of representatives on mission and the appointment of Ministers of Police and police officials had been steps in this direction, halting steps indeed when compared with the gigantic strides Napoleon took in his determination to strengthen and stabilize the state of France.

It would be very wrong to think of Napoleon only as a military dictator who made the model for the sinister regimes of Stalin, Mussolini, and Hitler. The Code Napoleon, that enduring body of civil law, among the components of which are a code of criminal procedure and a penal code, gave France for the first time a unitary system of law that was applicable equally to all citizens. It was not given only to France: many other countries in Europe, Asia, Africa, and the Americas have adopted it gladly.

Napoleon also gave France an effective Civil Service, which proved strong enough to survive the revolutions and rebellions of the nineteenth century and the political chaos of the twentieth. In Napoleonic administration a powerful and comprehensive system of police was of the utmost importance. Napoleon spent a great part of his time abroad; it has been calculated that during the ten years when he was emperor, he spent only 955 days in Paris, and he therefore had to have a firm and responsive surveillance and control of France independent of his personal direction.

For most of the Napoleonic era, the Minister of Police was Joseph Fouché. Minister of Police of the Consulate (1799–1802), Minister of Police of the Empire (1804–1810), he was recalled to the post for the Hundred Days in 1815 (and would be Minister of Police yet again under the restored Bourbon monarchy). Napoleon did not trust him but decided that he must employ this incredibly astute political master in his remaking of France. "He is the police incarnate," said the emperor, "he would teach it to God the Father and the devil would have nothing to teach him."

The Napoleonic Police System

While Napoleon took full advantage of the clean sweep the Revolution had made of the Ancien Regime's restrictive and obsolete practices in public administration, he was always ready to bring back anything that would serve the purposes of his emerging new state. The monarchy in 1789 had thirty-four Intendants of Justice, Police and Finance, "the king in the provinces." Napoleon revived the institution in much more trenchant form. The Revolution had divided France territorially into administrative departments; these now numbered ninety-eight, and over each of them Napoleon placed a prefect, nominated by himself, "the Emperor in miniature." Over the four or five *arrondissements* of each department, subprefects were placed. The central government also appointed the mayors. Each community of five thousand inhabitants was given a commissaire of police appointed by the central government and commissaires-general of police were appointed likewise for cities of 100,000 people. In a very short time Napoleon had imposed a police framework over the whole surface of France.

The framework was powerfully reinforced by the presence of the Gendarmerie. Napoleon delighted in the existence of this unique and time-tested force, which (as he wrote to Murat, King of Naples, in 1806) "provides the most efficacious means of maintaining the tranquillity of a country; it is a surveillance, half-civil, half-military, spread over the whole surface, and which makes the most precise reports." Napoleon augmented the force, raising its strength to some 30,000 by the end of his reign. He gave it prestige by placing it under the command of "a man I can trust, with a brilliant military reputation, an experienced man of unquestionable incorruptibility," General Moncey, soon to be a Marshal of the Empire. He gave it prestige, too, by using the Gendarmerie as fighting units on his campaigns as well as in their classical police role. It was the Gendarmerie, above all, who provided the police service for the departmental prefects.

The policing of Paris had fallen to a very low level during the Revolution, the National Guard and the civil police officials having proved inadequate to service the teeming, turbulent capital. It would have the fevered ambiance of a wartime capital, brilliant with uniforms, wild in its diversions, an unending carnival, throughout Napoleon's reign. One of his early acts, wisely, was to bring back in 1800 a police chief for Paris. The office of Lieutenant-General of Police, shorn of its judicial powers, was recreated under the title of Prefect of Police of Paris.

Over the whole police system brooded the Ministry of General Police, headed by the supreme exponent of the police art, Joseph Fouché, who would be rewarded in due course with a rich senatorship and the Dukedom of Otranto. The range of the Napoleonic police system can be glimpsed in the organization of Fouché's headquarters when it was fully developed.

Here were to be found the minister's cabinet and the general secretariat, through which all correspondence passed. Then came four divisions. The first dealt with matters concerning the security of the state and the policing of the interior of the state prisons. The second corresponded with senatorial commissions on the liberty of the individual and of the press. The third dealt with the administration of the amnesty granted to the *émigrés*, those who had left France since the Revolution and had returned or wished to return. The fourth dealt with the ministry's multifarious financial affairs, which included taxes on vice and gambling.

The ministry's archives collected, classified, and distributed all general police laws, decrees, and regulations, filed completed correspondence, and extracted information from it as necessary.

Four territorial divisions, each under a Councillor of State (i.e., a member of the Council appointed by Napoleon to prepare legislation, an élite body of forty), maintained ministerial surveillance of the police of the Empire, one for Paris, two for the provinces of France, and one for Italy.

This abstract summary of the ministry's headquarters arrangements gives only a faint idea of its activities and scope.

In police matters the departmental prefects as well as the Paris police prefect all answered to the minister and took directions from him. As far as public order was concerned, the Gendarmerie came under the minister and reported to him on many subjects. Napoleon, ruling by right of his own abilities and achievements, took every care to control public opinion; Fouché, unmatched in this field, oversaw much of his master's perpetual public-relations campaign. This involved harsh censorship of the press, the spreading of the right kinds of rumors, and the tracking down of spreaders of the wrong kinds, the commissioning of literary and artistic work and the publishing of such news, true or false, as Napoleon saw fit for his subjects to read. During the last months of the Directory, Fouché by his own account had suppressed 11 extremist journals of the Left and the Right. During the first year of the Consulate the number of Paris newspapers was cut from seventy-four to thirteen. During the Empire it was reduced to four, the leading one, *Le Moniteur,* being largely written by Fouché and other ministers. Its political articles had to be copied by the provincial press.

Napoleon, who made himself Emperor in 1804 and became more suspicious as he became more powerful, received domestic intelligence from many sources, notably from the Gendarmerie ("I am told only by Moncey of what is going on in France") and of course from Fouché's innumerable sources of information. Six nights a week, from the minister's cabinet, a secret bulletin was despatched to Napoleon, wherever he might be, so that he could, perhaps by the light of a campfire or in the state apartments of some defeated monarch, gauge the state of affairs in France.

The secret bulletins contain an extraordinary variety of information. Palace gossip, the audience's reaction to a new play, stock market prices, desertions from the army, arrests of foreign agents, results of interrogations, news of crime, offenses by soldiers, fires, rebellion against the gendarmerie, intercepted correspondence, visiting personages, public reception of news of victories, shipping news, indiscretions of Fouché's enemies, contractors' tenders, agitation against the draft, suicides, prison epidemics, progress of construction, unemployment figures, extracts from interministerial correspondence, persons detained or under special surveillance: the catalogue, good and bad, general and particular, goes on interminably, a kaleidoscope to be shaken into whatever pattern the emperor chose to find. P.-M. Desmarest, another former cleric, Fouché's chief intelligence aide, edited the bulletin and the minister added the final touches before sealing it and sending it on its way. The bulletins are the prototype of the reports of the General Intelligence branch of the Police Nationale today.

Fouché was a great master of intelligence and made signal contributions to the information Napoleon needed for his campaigns. He took what the emperor regarded as an undesirable interest in foreign affairs, in which he was deeply versed. He drew to the full upon his many and various personal contacts, systematically receiving information from the Empress Josephine (a connection dating back to before the coup d'état of Brumaire) and even from Napoleon's confidential secretary, Bourrienne. His resources were enormous. "All the state prisons were under my orders, as was the Gendarmerie. The granting of passports and visas belonged to me; I was charged with the surveillance of aliens, amnestied persons, *émigrés*. In the principal cities of the realm I established commissaires-general who extended, all over France, mainly on our frontiers, the network of the police." Fouché could not resist propagating the old police myth, any more than could de

Sartines before him: "I had the old police maxim revived, to wit that three men could not meet and talk indiscreetly about public affairs without the Minister of Police being informed about it the following day."

The State in Danger

Fouché, primarily concerned with his high police, was content to leave "whores, thieves and street-lamps" to the Prefect of Police, but when the need arose he could descend brilliantly from his heights to criminal police investigation. Such a need resulted from a "high police" emergency on Christmas Eve, 1800.

The First Consul was being driven in his coach to the Opera along the rue Saint-Nicaise when an infernal machine exploded. Napoleon's carriage was smashed and several of his suite killed. The device had been positioned and detonated with remarkable precision. Had the coach been driven at the usual speed, Napoleon would have been no more. The coachman, however, it is said, was more than somewhat inebriated and had driven faster than expected.

Napoleon, in a fury, was convinced that men of the Left, Jacobins, implacable revolutionaries, Fouché's former allies, were responsible for the outrage. In governmental circles, the minister's dismissal was confidently foretold. Fouché, imperturbable, vanished into his ministry to begin intensive inquiries. A reward was offered; the search began. The scene of the crime yielded a vital clue. The infernal machine had been in a horse-drawn cart. The horse had been destroyed in the explosion but it had been newly shod and one of its shoes showed that a hoof had been split. Inquiries among the Paris farriers turned up one who recognized the shoe and could describe the man who had brought the horse to him. A concerted sweep resulted in the arrest of one Carbon and six fellow conspirators. Fouché impassively presented the full proofs to the First Consul. The affair stood revealed as a royalist plot, financed by the English.

Despite the lingering menace of revolutionary fury over the middle classes' dominant position in the new France, the greatest danger was from the royalists, financed from their English and other bases outside France. The peasants of the West still yearned for church and king, and rebellion always smouldered there. One of Fouché's intelligence projects was concerned with them. He had caused a special "atlas" to be compiled, with data on each trouble spot and its inhabitants, which proved very useful to the officers of the Gendarmerie in their operations in the Vendée.

His view of the principle of collection and collation of information was expressed in a letter sent to all the departmental prefects in which he pointed out that an event unremarkable in the local context may be of great significance on a larger scale when related to kindred matters that would be locally unknown.

Throughout the period of the Empire, the war on espionage and subversion was waged remorselessly by the Ministry of Police. Spies were systematically hunted, arrested, court martialled, and shot. It was a time of war. An English visitor, John Carr, was impressed by the thoroughness of surveillance both in France and aborad. He wrote of "the promptitude and activity of the French police, under the penetrating eye of Mons. Fouché. No one can escape the vigilance of this man and his emissaries. An emigrant of respectability assured me, that when he and a friend waited upon him for their passports to enable them to quit Paris for the South of France, he surprised them by relating to them the names of the towns, the streets, and of the people with whom they had lodged, at various times, during their emigration in England."

During the Revolution France had become the land of the documented citizen: the passport and the identity card (even the words themselves) originated in France. The hotel and lodging-house registration of guests, the unending need to apply to the authorities for this and that, the official mania for keeping files on all and sundry, all this made it much easier for the police to lay hands on a particular person than it would have been in Britain or the United States.

Baron Hyde de Neuville, a dedicated and inveterately true royalist, proscribed by Bonaparte, writing at the time of the restoration of the Bourbon monarchy, took an understandably severe view of the Napoleonic police:

> I maintain that for twenty years there has been no Police in France. I cannot call Police a revolting inquisition, authorizing families to be

disturbed on the slightest suspicion, casting honest folk into irons, erecting scaffolds, ordering into exile, and finally raising and paying an army of secret agents designed to peddle falsehood and corrupt all classes of society by the vilest and most odious means. Such a Police requires neither great talent nor genius. To direct it, it suffices to have a hard heart, plenty of money and a great many slaves and wretches under one's orders.

He assessed the emperor's police chiefs, mentioning Savary, who succeeded Fouché as minister in 1810, and Dubois, the Prefect of Police of Paris, as "very mediocre men." He excepted Fouché (who indeed would have agreed with him about Savary and Dubois):

A man of intellect and very clever. Fouché did me great harm at a certain period of my persecution but later, won over either by my loyalty or the force of opinion, he sought to be helpful to my family.... What I can say of him is that at least he worked on *the grand scale.**

Policing

Very early in his tenure of office as Minister of Police of the Consulate, in 1799 Fouché sent a letter to the departmental prefects, enjoining them to be scrupulous in the discharge of their police responsibilities. It makes points of perennial interest:

Citizen Prefect, your connexions with justice are close and many. The relations between the actions of justice and the actions of police in fact impinge upon one another. They interpenetrate and appear to be confused one with the other. They continually concur in the same acts. Yet how often, in general, the concurrence is far from being an accord!

Surrounded with forms which it never finds sufficiently multiplied, justice has never forgiven police for its speed. Police, emancipated from almost all shackles, has never excused justice for its slowness. The reproaches they address to one another, society as a whole often addresses to them both.

*Excerpted and translated from a manuscript in the Archives Nationales, Paris, a copy of which was kindly communicated to me by my colleague, Professor John M. Cammett.

Police are reproached for harassing the innocent, justice for being unable to prevent or stop crime. Police, because it was in the king's hands, has generally been taken for an instrument of despotism.

Justice, because it is rendered by the organs of the laws, has often seemed to have gone astray amid their obscurities and contradictions....

What the positive orders of the law most imperatively command you, is not to hold any citizen in the hands of the police longer than is strictly necessary to place him in the hands of justice. The laws themselves make some exceptions to this law, the unique guarantee of all the others. These rare and well-defined exceptions the laws make with regret and almost with fear. If we were to add a single one, we should no longer be magistrates of police but agents of tyranny....

Never forget how dangerous it is to make arrests on mere suspicion; reflect that your actions, even when they are in error, will be a primary presumption against those whom you take before justice; and meditate in the quick of your conscience upon the history of so many innocent people who were sent by justice to the scaffold only because they were taken before justice in error.

The words come strangely from the terrorist emeritus, but the times had changed and, as Fouché commented, "everything changed with them." During the Empire the times went on changing. In 1810 the emperor's Privy Council was empowered to make punitive arrests of a year's duration. Administrative detention was a frequent recourse with the later Fouché, and his biographer, Louis Madelin, remarks that he "distributed more *lettres de chachet* than all the ministers of Louis XIV and Louis XV put togehter."

As far as the ordinary citizen was concerned, the main benefits of the Napoleonic police system were the benefits that can only accrue from methodical, regular, quotidian police work. During the Revolution crime had escalated in the absence of such a service, with robber bands roaming the countryside, terrorizing farmers and travellers, and the streets of the cities plagued by violence and vice. The only force that had carried on its police duties regularly and creditably was the Gendarmerie. Not until Bonaparte built the police into his centralized administration did Paris in particular and urban France in general recover any measure of the security that had been enjoyed under the Ancien Regime.

End of an Empire

Napoleon, the warrior, found his nemesis in war. After the Battle of Waterloo in 1815 he abdicated, Fouché being one of the prime movers in forcing his hand to do so. The emperor went to his last exile on the island of St. Helena in the South Atlantic. Fouché, who had contrived to have himself made Minister of Police of the restored royal government, this time fell quickly from favor and also went into exile, dying a millionaire duke on the Illyrian coast at Trieste.

The police system they left behind them is still the basic police system of France.

CHAPTER 5

The Nineteenth Century

In the 19th C.

Police in Uniform

 While the general structure of the police survived the fall of
Napoleon, the Ministry of Police, though retained for a short
period, was discontinued in 1818 and its functions were transferred to the Ministry of the Interior. Since then it has only once
been revived. With the departure of Fouché, the vibrant unity of
the imperial police system died. Its political mastery was lost and
localism eroded the firm framework of the machine.

The nineteenth century was to see a great deal of police development. The most evident feature of this was the evolution of
uniformed civil police. Several months before Robert Peel's Metropolitan Police appeared in the streets of London, sixteen years
before New York City had a similar force, an able Prefect of
Police, Louis-Marie Debelleyme, in 1829 put one hundred
policemen into blue uniforms and cocked hats, by day carrying a
cane, by night a saber, and set them to patrol the streets of the capital. One of the Prefect's officials wrote on the value of a civil
police uniform:

The purpose of uniform will be constantly to keep in the public's mind the presence of policemen at points where they will be of service; at the same time to compel them to intervene and restore order instead of vanishing into the crowd for fear of being noticed, as often happens.

To prevent habitual frequenting of taverns and persistence in bad habits, such as intemperance and gambling.

To constrain them to do their duty with regularity and, under constant control, to behave with composure and moderation.

There is one consideration of morale which is perhaps even more convincing, upon which I particularly insist, my duties having given me the opportunity of seeing its effect in various circumstances: that is the repugnance exhibited by the public to lending assistance, when it least expects to, at the request of a man who has no outward mark of his position.

Debelleyme selected officers who had been soldiers of good character and would look well in uniform. His orders in some respects resemble those issued a few months later to London's new police and in 1845 to the new police of New York:

> The success of this measure is assured if the *sergents de ville* [the name given to the men of this new corps: it means "city officer," the association with the military rank of sergeant being coincidental] cause themselves to be remarked by good bearing, regular conduct and honest and moderate words and deeds as far as the public is concerned.

The *sergents de ville* soon proved a success. They were to reach the height of their celebrity during the Second Empire of Napoleon III (1852–1870). They were the forerunners of the Police Nationale's present uniform branch, since 1871 known as the *gardiens de la paix* (guardians of the peace—very much akin to the name of the national police of the Republic of Ireland today, the Gárda Síochána).

During his short prefecture of eighteen months' duration, Debelleyme established the post of Chief of the Municipal Police, appointing Thouret, a man with his own sense of the police function. One of Thouret's early directives reads:

> Our municipal police has as its essential purpose the security of the inhabitants of Paris.

Thus, security by day and night, free and convenient movement, cleanliness of the streets, surveillance and precautions against all causes of accidents, maintenance of order in public places, seeking out crimes and their perpetrators: such will be the principal purposes of our solicitude and our constant and sustained care.

We shall concern ourselves solely with the inhabitants of Paris; it is for them that policing is being carried out. Our action with regard to the public will thus be benevolent without ceasing to be regular, constant and uniform.

That action will never assume the character of repression or of violence.

The police chiefs were doing better than the king. Charles X had embarked upon an intensely unpopular policy of reaction: Debelleyme was taking wise administrative measures. He abolished the infamous monthly tax that the prostitutes had been paying for the privilege of practicing the oldest profession. A valuable step was taken by the creation of a post of commissaires of police *aux délégations judiciaires,* whereby three commissaires were placed at the exclusive disposal of the judicial authorities responsible for the proofs and prosecution of crime. Debelleyme also instituted a fixed schedule for the city's public omnibus service. He could not, however, continue in office under a regime whose policies he deplored and which, as he warned, was rapidly engineering its own downfall, and in August 1829 he resigned. The ultra-royalist ministry replaced him with a headstrong lawyer of its own political persuasion, Jean Mangin.

Mangin reduced the *sergents de ville* by two-thirds and put the remainder into plain clothes. In July 1830, Charles X began to rule by ordinances, suspending the freedom of the press, dissolving the Chamber of Deputies, and altering the voting procedure. On July 26th the Prefect of Police sent his evening intelligence report* to the royal government:

General Surveillance
The most perfect tranquillity continues to reign at all points of the capital. No event worthy of special attention has been recorded in any of the reports which have reached me.

---

*Reproduced in Jean Tulard's *La Préfecture de Police sous la Monarchie de Juillet* (1964).

It was to be his last report. That very day, despite his reassuring news, the Paris journalists had published their remonstrance against the ordinances; in central Paris there had been cries for constitutional government and the dismissal of the ministry. The following day the barricades were up in the streets and the July Revolution had begun. Three days later, the monarchy fell.

The *sergents de ville* were soon missed. September 1830 would find them back on the streets again.

Charles X was succeeded by a member of the younger branch of the Bourbon family, King Louis-Philippe. France wearied of him and 1848 saw the barricades again, the king in flight, and a revolutionary government in power. The Second Republic began.

The new rulers replaced the *sergents de ville* with an improvised force of freedom fighters, the *Montagnards* (mountaineers, harking back to the extreme political party that sat on the highest benches of the National Convention); they did very well in the circumstances, for this was at first one of France's more humane revolutions. The republican Prefect of Police, Caussidière, kept the Prefecture's organization intact and even paid the salaries of the dispossessed *sergents de ville.* The government then decided to form a civil police force on the London model, but this project never came to fruition. In March 1849, the cocked hats and blue coats of the *sergents de ville* were back.

There they would remain until 1870. In 1852, the Second Republic having had a much shorter life than the First, for its first and only president had been Louis-Napoleon Bonaparte, nephew of the emperor, and he established a Second Empire. In exile in England, the future Napoleon III (Napoleon I's son died young) took a great interest in the police and even served as a special constable (auxiliary policeman) during the Chartist troubles in London in 1848. Once enthroned, Napoleon III made much of his uniformed police, and the *sergents de ville* with their imperial beards and sabers made a brave show in the streets of Paris.

Maxime du Camp, in his six-volume description of Paris during the Second Empire, wrote:

Who does not know the *sergents de ville?* Who has not seen them taking up position on the boulevards to bring some order into the traffic, pacing slowly along our streets, mounting guard outside their stations? Who has not noticed their uniform, in winter a long greatcoat, in summer a clumsy frock-coat on the collar of which, in silver embroidery, appear the number of their division, the letter of their squad and a number which, being personal to them, invariably enables responsibility for their actions to be brought home to them?

Street duty was hard on them, du Camp found. Only 20 percent completed the twenty-five years necessary to qualify for pension. Their usual tour of duty was eight hours.

> The inevitable irregularity of meal-times, the sudden changes of temperature when a man returns to the station after patrol, the need to keep on wet clothes on rainy days, the long and exhausting tours on bridges and at intersections in wind, sun, hail and snow, eventually break down the most robust constitution and bring to hospital beds men who looked like living to be a hundred.

The rigors of foot patrol have not changed all that much in the past two centuries, though the modern counterparts of the *sergents de ville* have far fewer days on duty and far more chances of promotion or assignment to other work.

When du Camp wrote, at the end of the Second Empire, the corps of *sergents de ville* had grown from Debelleyme's pioneer 100 to 3,864 men. The Metropolitan Police of London at that time had a total strength of 8,963, most of whom were in uniform; New York City had 2,000 patrolmen.

In 1864, the Prefect of Police, Joachim Piétri, having studied the organization at Scotland Yard, divided up the work of his own headquarters on similar lines and adopted the London system of beat patrol round the clock, assigning both uniformed and plainclothes police to specific areas so that they could get to know the neighborhood.

Napoleon III's military heritage proved too much for him. In 1870 he went to war with Prussia, was badly beaten, and abdicated. The war continued. In September of that year, the Prefect of Police, de Kératry, disbanded nearly all the uniformed police to reinforce the army and patrolled Paris with the remaining three hundred of them, renamed *gardiens de la paix*. The corps of *gardiens* was quickly built up again by reemploying the former *sergents de ville*. The fighting with the Prussians ceased when Paris capitulated in January 1871. The police, scapegoats for the discredited imperial regime, execrated by the populace, had nevertheless fought bravely in the front line in the defense of the city. Now a new ordeal awaited them: the Commune.

The Prussians made their victorious entry into Paris on March 1, 1871, marching out again on March 4th. The populace, infuriated by this humiliation, turned on the government's most visible representatives, the police. The Leftist insurrection, dreaded by the bourgeoisie ever since the first Revolution, now flared. Thiers, head of the provisional government, ordered the removal of the administration from Paris to the comparative security of Versailles. Police and troops covered the withdrawal, moving after the government, but many policemen were left in the city, where they subsequently proved a valuable source of intelligence. Paris was now under the revolutionary Central Committee, with the volunteer National Guard as its police force. This was now civil war.

The Versailles government sent in the army, over 100,000 troops, on May 21st. Street fighting on barricades, a week's hand-to-hand struggle, merciless on both sides, culminated in bloody and protracted reprisals by the victorious government. Casualties were some 25,000 Parisians killed (the Versailles force lost less than 1,000) either in battle or by summary execution. More people died during the repression of the Commune in a single week of May 1871, than had died during the whole period of the Terror in 1794.

Elections in 1871 decided that France should have a Third Republic and the *gardiens de la paix* resumed the uniform patrolling of Paris.

In 1889 conditions of entry to the corps were laid down. Candidates must be natives or naturalized citizens of France, under thirty years of age (thirty-five in the case of ex-soldiers), at least five feet, six inches in height, able to read and write easily, Paris residents, physically fit and of good character, and able to pass an entrance examination set and graded by the Prefecture of Police. Since 1883 there had been a training school for recruits to the force, where they were regularly instructed in handwriting, arithmetic, report writing, relations with the public, discipline, law, drill, and weaponry (rifle, saber-bayonet, revolver).

The year 1893 saw the appointment of one of the really outstanding Prefects of Police. Louis Lépine, at first derisively but soon admiringly called "the Prefect of the streets," incarnated the Anglo-American stereotype of the time of the Frenchman: small, bearded, in derby hat and tail coat, emphatic of gesture, and mercurial of temperament. The spry, game little man delighted in being with his men in any kind of action—strikes, demonstrations, fires, arrests of dangerous terrorists all brought him out to the scene at any hour of the day or night. He had great qualities of leadership and provides a perfect case study of how the character, personality, and talents of an individual can mould the character of a large organization. He was determined to make the Parisian populace like their police and equally determined to make the police proud of themselves. Bad morale of long standing was overcome by the inspiration of Lépine's wholehearted love of what he was doing and by the decisive, sincere, and considerate way in which he exercised his high command. He had the advantage of being long in office, from 1893, with a break from 1897 to 1899, until 1913. He brought Paris's police in good heart into the new century.

Criminal Investigation

The Paris police in the nineteenth century were generally regarded as having the world's best detective organization. Their obvious competitors, in London and New York City, had begun with the need to establish a police image free from any suspicion of domestic espionage and administrative interference, both ancient and accepted elements of French policing, and the open, uniformed police style was adopted at the expense of investigative functions. The Paris police had the rigorous documentation of the citizen and his readily ascertained identity and movements as an invaluable detective resource. They had, moreover, the benefit of the long-established mystique of police omniscience, something that was certainly not then enjoyed by police in New York or London. It was quite natural for Edgar Allan Poe, writing in the 1840s, to make the first of fiction's great detectives, Dupin (a prototype of Sherlock Holmes), a Frenchman living in Paris.

The legendary fame of the Paris detectives began with Vidocq.

His memoirs (ghosted) and many books, even plays, about him, his acquaintance with the great novelist Balzac, who is believed to have based one of the key characters in his Human Comedy series, Vautrin, master of the underworld, upon him, propagated the notoriety of a man whose real life was very remarkable. Vidocq was recruited by Monsieur Henry, the astute head of the criminal division of the Prefecture of Police towards the end of the First Empire, while he was a prisoner on the run from penal servitude. Henry used him first as a *mouton,* an informer inside the prisons, where he produced such good results that he was released to form a small detective unit for the police.

In those days the detective work in Paris was largely in the hands of the twenty-four *officiers de paix,* each with a few men under him, working independently in their own areas. This put criminal investigation on a very local basis and it was Monsieur Henry's intention to remedy this by having a central detective squad that would work anywhere in the city and report not to the local commissaires of police but to him.

Vidocq employed ex-criminals who had served their sentences as his detective agents and rewarded them according to their results. Backed by his unique knowledge of the criminal world (he had twice been imprisoned for substantial periods in the galleys, where the worst offenders were sent) and his great courage, intuition, doggedness, and powers of analysis, the new unit soon proved its worth. Napoleonic and Restoration Paris was relieved of many predators. Vidocq's organization, building up a record system, developing techniques, became an established feature of the criminal division and acquired the name of "the *Sûreté,*" and until 1913, when it became the *Police Judiciaire,* the detective branch of the Prefecture of Police continued to operate under that title.

In 1832, the Prefect of Police, Gisquet, decided it was time to rehabilitate the *Sûreté.* It had something of a reputation for using the ruses of the *agent-provocateur* (another French contribution to the vocabulary of criminal justice) and the criminal records of some of its agents could be injurious to a prosecution case. Gisquet therefore staffed it with regular police officers (Vidocq had had to pay his men from the Prefecture's secret funds) and put it under Pierre Allard, a commissaire of police who had to forfeit his magisterial status and step down to the rank of *officier de paix* to take the job, with Louis Canler as his chief inspector. There were four *brigadiers* (sergeants), twenty-one *inspecteurs* (detectives), and four clerks. The branch was now placed under the Chief of the Municipal Police.

Despite all the talk of rehabilitation, those who had to do the detective work soon realized that they had to have underhand contact with crime. The old saying that a detective is as good as his informers was appreciated. Canler, who succeeded Allard as Chief of the *Sûreté* in 1848 wrote in his memoirs: "I resolved to form a squad of informers.... I recruited recently-convicted criminals and put them under regular discipline. Each of them was well rewarded." He also employed ex-convicts who had broken the residence stipulation of their parole to come and live in Paris.

The work of the vice squad is distinct from that of the detectives (though it was incorporated in the *Sûreté* in 1881) but prostitutes have always been a source of criminal information. The plain-clothes branch of the Paris police had been regulating prostitution since the Middle Ages and in the pleasure capital of nineteenth-century Europe it was kept busy. The Prefect of Police stated that in 1894, 26,000 women were arrested as prostitutes; it was reckoned that 40,000 women were so employed. Since the Ancien Régime the police had registered prostitutes and continued to do so until 1946. The Prefecture's medical dispensary had a staff of doctors who conducted regular medical examinations. The brothel was a recognized institution; Sir Francis Head, writing in the middle of the nineteenth century, noted:

> No house of bad conduct is allowed, as in England, of its own accord to fester up and break out wherever it likes; but such evils, which it is deemed advisable not altogether to prevent, are licensed to exist in certain localities, and are forbidden from others, especially from the vicinity of any school, public institution, or church. From the instant they are established the exterior and interior are placed under the constant and especial surveillance of a particular department of the police, the regulations of which appear to have no other object than despotically reduce to the minimum the list of evils consequent upon that which, if not implanted, has deliberately been allowed to take root. For instance, each mistress of a house of this description is obliged, within twenty-four hours, to bring with her to be enregis-

tered at the prefecture of police every female who may be desirous to live with her. On her arrival there, the delinquent is seriously admonished to relinquish her intention; and to induce, or rather to terrify and disgust her, she is informed in detail of the surveillance to which she will be subjected. If the candidate is very young, instead of this course she is, in the first instance, carried from the brink of ruin to the hospital of St. Lazare, where work is given to her, and endeavours are made to reclaim her. If from the country, a letter is addressed by the police to her parents or nearest relatives, informing them of her position, and urging them to save her. If no answer be received, and if her friends cannot be found out, a letter is written to the mayor of her commune, requesting him to endeavour to do so. If her friends decline to come forward, or if it be ascertained that she is friendless, a last effort is made in the hospital of St. Lazare to reclaim her, and if *that* proves to be in vain, her name is then irrevocably inscribed; and, destitute of character and of liberty, she passes the remainder of her life under the dreadful appellation of *"une fille inscrite."* Not only is every change of her domicile recorded in the books of the police, but on the ticket she is obliged to bear,—and which at any hour and by any person she may be required to produce—there must be inscribed the results of the weekly professional visits to which she is subjected.

The memoirs of G. Macé, Chief of the *Sûreté* from 1879 to 1884, vividly evoke the old detective service. It was in his time that the branch was established in its present home, the celebrated 36, quai des Orfèvres, on the Ile de la Cité. In those days, it would appear from his account, morale was poor. Louis-Napoleon's much publicized detectives under the famous Monsieur Claude (whose ghosted memoirs are not to be relied upon), having benefited perhaps from imperial propaganda, are hard to reconcile with Macé's disillusioned description of a down-trodden service. Yet the work was done, as work so often is in the most adverse circumstances, the detectives's self-respect more than the poor material reward being the decisive factor. Few, according to Macé, reached the pensionable stage; resignations, dismissals, bronchitis from the winter tours of street duty, cut careers short. The reporting of crime to the *Sûreté* by way of the leisurely offices of the Municipal Police was ridiculously slow. It took the Civil Service system two days to get a specially urgent case to the Chief, the usual delay being a week. Macé, campaigning to have the *Sûreté* made a department in its own right rather than a branch of the Municipal Police, resigned in despair. The reform he sought, whereby the Chief of the *Sûreté* would be allowed to report directly to the Cabinet of the Prefect of Police, was implemented in 1887.

One of Macé's successors, Goron, who was appointed to the post in that year, also wrote highly informative memoirs of the service. He was astonished to find that as few as 350 men were holding the line against the crime of Paris. Recruited on the basis of military certificates and the recommendation of a minister or a member of the legislature, the new detective served no probationary period. Once he was in, however little aptitude he showed, the regulations made it hard to get him out. Of the total strength of 350, many were required for administrative and clerical duties in the headquarters, especially in connection with criminal records, and many were needed to make "family" inquiries, "missing persons," a frequent activity in the interests of the most important unit of French society. The exterior services included the "street" section, whose agents roamed Paris in search of pickpockets, shoplifters, burglars, sneak thieves, and robbers, watching over the big storefronts, the race courses, and even the charity boxes in the churches. In 1888 the section made some 2,500 arrests. The most famous unit of the *Sûreté* was "the Chief's squad," to which fell the most dangerous and important cases, the kind of work done in modern detective fiction by Georges Simenon's excellent character, Maigret.

If the detective branch in Paris had its troubles, in 1877 its counterpart in London was by no means immune from them. The shock of four of the most senior detective officers at Scotland Yard being charged for collusion with race-course swindlers led to an official inquiry into the management of the Detective Department. An enterprising young barrister, Howard Vincent, having reason to believe that detective work was one of the things they managed better in France, crossed the Channel to study the Paris system. The Prefect of Police was most helpful and Vincent was able on his return to London to submit a meticulous report to the authorities. This was favorably received, with the result that Vincent was appointed to direct the newly organized Criminal Investigation Department, established in 1878. It bore a marked resemblance to the centralized *Sûreté*.

At about the time of Howard Vincent's visit to the Prefecture of Police, Alphonse Bertillon was appointed there as a records clerk. The unpromising son of a scientific family, he would soon be a more celebrated scientist than any of them. Within a year, disgusted by the vague and inefficient way in which the criminal records were kept, he put forward a scheme for identifying criminals by taking certain measurements of the adult body, holding that these would result in a formula unique to each individual. Initially rebuffed by one Prefect of Police, who threatened to fire him, but provisionally encouraged by his successor, Bertillon succeeded in 1883 in identifying his first recidivist, one of 43 in that year, while in 1884 he made 241 identifications. It was a great scientific breakthrough in police work. The anthropometric ("man-measurement") system was the first scientific method of identifying a criminal ever used by any police force.

Fingerprinting, which largely superseded it, was not used by police until its experimental introduction in Bengal, India, by E.R. Henry, who was to bring it into operation at New Scotland Yard in 1901. It is scarcely possible to overrate Bertillon's contribution to police development. The anthropometric file of crucial measurements and other data brought precision into what had always hitherto been a very hit-or-miss business. The memory of police and prison officers, of victims, and of other witnesses had been the principal hope of identifying any criminal who was not caught red-handed. Criminals had known from time immemorial that change of name and location would often guarantee immunity. In its perfected form, as Henri Souchon points out in his essay in *Pioneers in Policing,* the Bertillon file "permits a rapid search by reason of the mathematical series of measurements, allows an easy follow-up through the near-perfect description of the *portrait parlé,* facilitates recognition by the witness on account of the photography and makes possible the judiciary identification by particular marks and fingerprints." The *portrait parlé* ("speaking likeness") consisted of full-face and profile photographs, with precise and systematic description in words of physical characteristics. It is still part of police identification technique, although the volume of work has led to simplifications that have robbed it of its original comprehensiveness and exactitude.

The anthropometric system had fundamental problems, however, one of the greatest being that of uniformity in measurement: one prison officer might squeeze the calipers tighter than another, for instance, and it had the great disadvantage of not being applicable to persons who were not fully grown, thus excluding all juvenile offenders. The system was discredited in the United States in 1903 when one Will West, after being anthropometrically measured in the federal prison at Leavenworth, Kansas, was identified as a previous convict called William West. Comparison of fingerprints established that a different man was concerned and this was proved up to the hilt when it was found that the other West was serving a sentence in the prison at the time.

Bertillon's claim to fame does not rest upon anthropometry alone. Police laboratories all over the world are indebted to his many inventions and techniques. He was a great pioneer of police photography—at the scene of crime, particularly—and of such criminalistic matters as handwriting and forgery analysis, ballistics, galvanoplastic preservation of footprints, the dynamometer used for measuring the degree of force used in housebreaking and the "Bertillon kit," the case of equipment that detectives take to the crime scene.

In handwriting, as in anthropometry, though more spectacularly, Bertillon incurred adverse publicity when he came down on the wrong side in the century's most resounding trial. He identified the key incriminating document in the Dreyfus Case as being in the handwriting of the defendant, Captain Dreyfus, who was finally exonerated.

Bertillon must not only be regarded as having provided police with the means of catching offenders. Before his time, the rudimentary, haphazard ways of identifying suspects as criminals must have resulted in innumerable miscarriages of justice: in the present age the unreliability of eyewitness identification has been frequently demonstrated. Bertillon's contribution was probably even more valuable in vindicating the innocent than in convicting the guilty. In any case, it was Bertillon who established once and for all the use of science by the police.

So, in France, the great nineteenth-century development of the natural sciences found its place in criminal justice. In this connection should be mentioned also the contribution of a French medical doctor, Mathieu Orfila (1787–1853) who first proved in court the presence of arsenic in a murder victim. A much greater event was the founding in Lyon of the criminalistic laboratory by the medico-legist, Jean-Alexandre Lacassagne, in 1884. Lacassagne could rise superior, too, to his own specialisms. Addressing the Conference of Criminal Anthropology in Rome two years later, he said:

> The social milieu is also important. Perhaps you will allow me to borrow an analogy from a modern theory. The social milieu is the culture-broth of criminality; the microbe is the criminal, an element which has no importance until it finds the medium in which it can grow.... Societies get the criminals they deserve.

Centralization

It was not until the middle of the nineteenth-century that "high police" (however ineptly it was carried on) and initiatives of centralization of police resources at the national level were revived. Napoleon III, conscious of the precariousness of his Second Empire, took measures to be better informed and to have more control of the provincial cities than had the kings who had reigned between 1815 and 1848.

He partly owed his imperial throne, indeed, to police complicity. The Prefect of Police of the Second Republic, Carlier, did not seem sufficiently enthusiastic in Napoleon's cause, so he appointed one of his disciples, Charlemagne de Maupas, to replace him, on the understanding that the new Prefect would facilitate a coup d'état. He was given half a million francs, as were the Ministers of War and the Interior.

De Maupas summoned his forty-eight commissaires of police to the Prefecture at 3.00 A.M. on December 2, 1851, and all but one (who was immediately locked up) assisted the Prefect to arrest about eighty members of the parliamentary opposition and anyone else who might be dangerous; they were removed to prison. The Army supported the nephew of the great Napoleon and a plebiscite confirmed the conspirator-president as the Emperor Napoleon III. It may be recalled that the first Napoleon came to power as First Consul in 1799 by a coup d'état to which the Minister of Police had been no stranger.

De Maupas exacted the revival of the Ministry of Police for his services but he held it only for a short time and totally without distinction. The oversight of the police reverted to the Ministry of the Interior, whence it was removed and entrusted to the Prefect of Police from 1859 to 1870. Another reversion to the Ministry of the Interior was followed by the Prefect of Police regaining it from 1874 to 1876. Thereafter it remained with the Ministry of the Interior.

In 1851 the police of France's largest provincial city, Lyon, was made a national police force, financed from the budget of the central government. The police powers of the mayor passed to the departmental prefect, the Prefect of the Rhône. It was the only provincial police force so subsidized; all the others, and also the police of Paris, were municipally supported. American and English readers may be surprised at the degree of power the Paris government exercised over the provincial police—appointing the chiefs of police in every case, at so little expense to the national purse. In 1854 the imperial administration strengthened its hold by appointing central (supervisory) commissaires in all the larger urban centers where there was more than one commissaire of police. They were responsible to the prefects of their respective departments.

The coming of the railways gave a new and dangerous mobility to criminals and, in the imperial view, an even more dangerous mobility to conspirators. Ostensibly to exercise surveillance over railway passengers and railway stations, a Special Railway Police (*Police spéciale des chemins de fer*) was created by imperial decree in 1855, under the Minister of the Interior—a police service of the central government. There were originally thirty commissaires of police, six stationed in Paris, two in Lyon, and the rest singly at the more important railway stations. To assist them there were seventy *inspecteurs*. The commissaires were to report both to the prefect of their department and to the Minister of the Interior. A central commissaire was appointed to coordinate the service. The ordinary police role of the commissaires was stressed to disguise that the real purpose of these new police officials was to collect political intelligence. It is clear from the orders issued at the time that the security of the state was the motive for the measure. The word *Sûreté* now began to have an additional and wider meaning in the police vocabulary, distinct from its use in connection with the detective branch of the Prefecture of Police, signifying the central police organisms housed in the Ministry of the Interior.

No one has a greater fear of conspiracies than a conspirator who has come into power. Napoleon III also caused the Prefecture of Police to form a political branch under a commissaire of police, Lagrange. Lavishly financed from secret funds, the branch had three groups, each comprising twenty *inspecteurs* under an *officier de paix*.

Despite the existence of all these security police, a visit to the Opera proved as nearly fatal to his nephew as it nearly was in 1800 to Napoleon I. Felice Orsini and two other Italian refugees threw grenades at the emperor's carriage. Napoleon III and his consort escaped unhurt but 8 people were killed and 148 injured. Better police work could surely have prevented this crime, for Orsini was known as a dangerous conspirator and he and his associates had traveled from England to make their attempt. The Paris police and the Ministry of the Interior, with all their control resources, should have been aware of their presence in the capital. Napoleon III was of this opinion, for he dismissed the minister and the Prefect of Police.

The Second Empire began the movement to restore the centralization of the police that the First Empire had instituted, its watchword for the measures it took being "the security of the State." Much more importance was attached to keeping Napoleon III in power than to the basic purposes of police work. The police even provoked riots so that the imperial government could have the credit for putting them down. The departmental prefects' best efforts were political rather than administrative, being directed to ensuring favorable results at election times. As a police state, the Second Empire was a very second-class version of the First. The popular explosion that came in 1871 demonstrated how ineffective its "high police" had been in understanding and controlling the political forces at work beneath the surface.

The problem of the central control of the police led, as mentioned above, to a variety of ephemeral solutions. In 1881 it was the responsibility of the Minister of the Interior, whose administration was mainly organized in respect of the supervision of local government throughout France. It was therefore decided to create a special organization within the ministry to supervise the police. In 1881 the decision was implemented by the creation of a new directorate, the *Sûreté Générale* (General Security). A decree of 1885 instituted Controllers-General, with offices in the ministry, to supervise and report on the performance of the police.

In 1894, France entered upon a security nightmare. Captain Dreyfus, of the *Deuxième Bureau* of the Army, was court martialled for high treason, charged with having given secret information to Germany. As the *Deuxième Bureau*'s responsibilities included counterespionage, the case was particularly grave. The Dreyfus Affair made history for many reasons, ending some twelve years later with the exoneration of Captain Dreyfus, but one of its solutions was for the counterespionage service to be transferred from the Army to the police. A new police branch came into being in 1899: the *Surveillance du Territoire* (surveillance of the country), to deal with espionage within the frontiers of France.

During the latter part of the nineteenth century the centralization of police power proceeded by focusing in the Ministry of the Interior the general oversight of the police and the particular control of specialist police branches.

The Gendarmerie

Whatever the difficulties of maintaining control of France's multifarious police organizations in the civil sphere, there was always one powerful police force under the control of the central government: the Gendarmerie Nationale.

As noted in the previous chapter, Napoleon had the highest regard for the force. During the Consulate he built it up to 2,500 squads, each of six gendarmes, the whole forming 27 legions. During the Empire the strength rose. The high command comprised a marshal of the Empire, two divisional generals, and four brigadier-generals, with forty legions in France, Belgium, and the Low Countries. The cost of finding barracks fell entirely upon departmental budgets (until 1931), an arrangement highly congenial to the central government.

During the First Empire the Gendarmerie was employed on secret and political missions, involving the use of civilian clothing and disguises. This alienated the public and after Napoleon I's fall, the royal government laid it down in an ordinance of 1820 that the Gendarmerie would perform all its duties "openly in military uniform, without actions susceptible of injuring consideration of the Arm and abstaining from any secret missions of a nature to rob it of its true character."

The practice of stationing a Gendarmerie formation in Paris stems, more than somewhat indirectly, from the ancient *Guet,* the royal military watch of the capital. This force, consolidated with the Paris Guard during the late eighteenth century, was succeeded by the Municipal Guard of 1802, which was replaced in 1815 by the Royal Gendarmerie of Paris, distinguished from its predecessors by being drawn entirely from units of the Gendarmerie. In 1849 it was renamed the Republican Guard of Paris; during the Second Empire it became the Paris Guard; from 1870 it was the Republican Guard of Paris. Since the First Empire the Guard has been in varying degrees at the disposal of the Prefect of Police of Paris.

The performance of the Gendarmerie's normal day-to-day police duties was inhibited during the First Empire by its participation in Napoleon's campaigns, by the diversion of its energies into political channels, and by having to meet the danger of civil war in the West. For the rest of the century, apart from the dislocations consequent upon violent changes of the regime, the Gendarmerie was free to continue with its classical mission. The 1820 ordinance quoted above provided that the force would be solely under military command.

Between 1820 and 1830 its numbers fell. Grave problems of public order engaged it during the fall of the Bourbon Monarchy in 1830, the revolution bringing in the Second Republic in 1848, and the disturbances caused by the coup d'état in 1851. In 1854 a decree laid down the organization again, reaffirming the exclusive control of the Minister of War and the prohibition of secret missions. It confirmed the force's jurisdiction over all offenses. The Gendarmerie continued to add to its battle honors, fighting in the Crimea in 1855, and the defense of Paris against the Prussians in 1870–1871. In the latter year, a Legion of Mobile Gendarmerie was formed, forerunner of the Gendarmerie Mobile of today.

In his rural police role, the nineteenth-century gendarme

acquired a certain reputation for brusqueness and inflexibility in his dealings with the erring citizen in matters great and small, especially small. The military mind does not always adapt well to the wilful world outside the barrack gates. The dramatist Courteline's *Le Gendarme est sans pitié*, produced at the Théâtre Antoine in Paris in 1899, reflects popular feeling in its story of how a local public prosecutor, plagued to death by the incessant reports of an officious gendarme, eventually gets the better of him by beating him at his own game. Whatever else the nineteenth-century gendarme may have inspired, however, he always inspired respect.

It would seem that in the later part of the century the Gendarmerie's organization was strained by being too thinly spread. The increase in mobile crime, including the ravages of innumerable vagabonds, suggests that the force had become too localized in its outlook.

CHAPTER 6

Police Development: 1900–1945

Regional Crime Squads

The *Sûreté Générale* (which became the *Sûreté Nationale* in 1934) had developed during the later nineteenth century into the supervisory organization of the police of the provinces. Understaffed for the purpose and remote from the ordinary police of the urban centers, the *Sûreté* now found itself faced with a serious increase in mobile crime, on a nationwide scale. Its resources were unequal to the needs of the situation.

The civil police of the provinces, very much under municipal influences, were untrained save by the experience they gained in the course of their work, and were inevitably parochial in outlook. Their superiors, the commissaires of police, though appointed at the national level, were equally lacking in professional preparation and usually became immersed in local business, taking little interest in what happened outside their own territory. In 1900 only the police of Lyon, under direct prefectoral supervision, were really integrated into the *Sûreté's* system. The Gendarmerie, highly visible in its military uniforms, implanted since a decree reorganizing

73

it in 1903 in over 3,600 communities in small squads, provided a mainly preventive police on a localized basis, while being able to provide mobile forces in the event of public disorder.

Crime was not slow to take advantage of the shortcomings of the police. As Melville Lee, historian of the English police, wrote at about this time: "Crime follows impunity." Criminal gangs proved particularly troublesome. In the North, at Hazebrouck, between 1904 and 1906 a gang committed 104 robberies and 8 murders; they were caught, but only because the brother of the leader of the fifty-nine-member gang informed against them. An Abbéville gang, some thirty in number operating in the Paris and Picardy region, committed over one hundred crimes. In the Southwest, the Boudhary gang, whose leader ran the railway restaurant at Langon, committed depredations on a similar scale, while from 1905 to 1908 ten robbers terrorized the Southeast region, pillaging the peasants and holding them to ransom. Nomadic bands roamed over the whole countryside, going from one market or fair to another, living off all kinds of robbery, theft, and trickery.

Fortunately, at this critical time, the right men were in the right places. Georges Clemenceau, who was to be France's great minister in the First World War, was Minister of the Interior and he had appointed a professional police officer to be Director of the *Sûreté*. Célestin Hennion had entered the service as one of the Special Commissaires of the Railway Police in 1883 and now, with much meritorious service and Clemenceau's vigorous support, he realized that it was up to him to tackle a crime wave, the like of which had not been seen since the banditry that had been the scourge of the countryside in revolutionary days. The coming of the automobile by no means coincidentally accompanied the rise in serious "professional" crime.

In 1907 Hennion assigned Jules Sébille, chief of the detective branch of the police of Lyon, to form and head a new police branch, the *brigades mobiles de police judiciaire* (mobile squads of detective police: the nearest English equivalent is "regional crime squads," a form of detective policing adopted by the British in the mid-1960s). The branch came into legal being on the last day of 1907.

There were to be twelve squads, with the mission of seeking out and repressing crime. The detectives' jurisdiction would be regional, as opposed to the municipal limits within which the existing investigative officers had to work, thus extending their range against the mobile criminal. They were enjoined to regard themselves as unifying and liaison elements of the whole criminal police effort, ensuring a flow of information to and from urban and other police and to the *Sûreté*'s headquarters, where records would be centralized. Bertillon at the Prefecture of Police promised close cooperation; a direct telephone line was to be installed between the *Sûreté* headquarters and his department.

Seasoned police officer as he was, Sébille was careful to caution the new police branch against treading on the toes of the local police. The regional crime squads' business was to supply what was deficient in the police effort, not to duplicate what was already being done adequately. Sébille, in the first flush of enthusiasm, preached that their mission was not merely repressive; they were to act preventively, by making sudden descents on the fairs and markets where the malefactors were likely to congregate. Objection, however, was taken to this: the true function of the squads was repressive. Their preventive impact would depend on the quality of their arrests, depriving some criminals of the liberty to commit offenses and thus warning others of what the consequences of crime would be. Observation was to be one of their priorities; they could go anywhere on their own initiative to identify and photograph members of criminal groups.

Originally the regional crime squads were small and they were warned not to waste their time on routine business. The senior officer of the squad would be a divisonal commissaire, because liaison had to be maintained with prefects, mayors, chiefs of urban police, and officers of the Gendarmerie. Hennion envisaged the squad chief as a kind of director of detective work for his whole region. Under him he would have two commissaires and ten *inspecteurs*. Stressing the importance of interchange of information between regions, Hennion said he would judge the service as a whole by the sum of its results rather than by the achievements of individual squads. He also began a *Bulletin of Criminal Police*, giving details of criminals, which came to be circulated throughout the police service.

The success of these anticrime units, with their element of mobility and extended jurisdiction may be measured by the government's readiness to augment them. By 1919 the original twelve squads had been increased to seventeen. In 1939 the officers of the squads were given nationwide jurisdiction. They had the opportunity, too rare in the public service, of initiative, being able to move freely in the course of their inquiries and to exercise their powers independently. They were closely linked with the public prosecutors of their areas and they were not overloaded, as were the detectives of the urban forces, with routine criminal work. In their first five years the regional crime squads made three thousand arrests.

A great statesman, Clemenceau, had for a moment concentrated his attention on crime. The result was a nationwide system of criminal investigation, the longest step forward the police had taken towards effective centralization since the First Empire.

General Intelligence

Yves Guyot said that in France the citizen is free to do what he likes—under police supervision. This is certainly true of gambling in France. Racecourses have been policed since 1891, originally by the Special Police of the Railways. The first police officer to be effective in this work, with particular reference to the Pari-Mutuel (Totalisator), was none other than Commissaire Célestin Hennion. Casinos, also a subject of police concern, caused much confusion in the legislative and administrative spheres but in 1907, when they were laid under contribution by the state, casinos and gambling clubs were licensed and placed under police surveillance, together with the race courses, thus justifying a special department of police work. This today comes under the Directorate of General Intelligence and Gambling (*Direction des renseignements généraux et des jeux*).

The practice of gathering information for the government, as has already been abundantly demonstrated, is an ancient one in France. Well established during the Ancien Regime, it was brought to a fine art by Fouché during the First Empire and revived by Napoleon III when he created the Special Police of the Railways. From that Special Police developed the important and substantial branch of the Police Nationale mentioned at the end of the last paragraph.

Marcel Sicot (later to be Secretary-General of Interpol) served as a Special Commissaire between the two World Wars, as he recalls in his memoirs, *Servitude et Grandeur Policieres*. Posted to Beauvais in 1924, despite his impressive rank, he found himself without even a typewriter in a tiny office between the reception desk and the toilets. He discovered that he was also in charge of counterespionage for the department, both functions—information and security—being performed by the Special Police until the reconstitution of the counterespionage service in 1934. In addition to these functions he was from time to time dispatched to deal with public-order situations when no other commissaire of police was available. Moreover, whenever public order was thought to be in peril in any part of the department, the Prefect would send him to act as his representative and liaison officer to concert measures with the mayor and the local police. There were no "office hours" or weekly rest days for the Special Commissaire. The Special Police often deplored the political nature of their work, which made them particularly vulnerable to the disfavor of influential people, and envied their colleagues who were employed in "ordinary" police duties.

The year 1936 found Marcel Sicot installed as chief of detectives at Versailles, prefectoral headquarters of the Department of Seine-et-Oise. He was astonished to find himself also in charge of the police of information. The two functions were hard to reconcile:

> In detective policing, one tackles tangible matters, one confirms or one reports concrete and precise facts on one's own responsibility. General Intelligence has to measure unmeasurable public opinion, seek to foresee its reactions and establish notes packed with prudent and conditional formulae.

During the Second World War, when France was occupied by the Germans and the Vichy government of Marshal Pétain was in power, the General Intelligence branch was constrained to act as the political police of the regime. This resulted in many resignations and much secret activity to protect persons threatened by deportation or hostage taking and on behalf of the Resistance. It also resulted in some fatal outcomes for the officers concerned. In 1944 General Intelligence resumed its proper mission of providing political, social, and economic intelligence for the information of the republican government.

Counterespionage

Counterespionage (*Surveillance du Territoire*) was entrusted to the police in 1899, but the military had never been pleased by having it taken away from them and had continued their own activities in this field. In 1934 police counterespionage was forced into greater activity as the Fascist powers' aggressive intelligence operations on French soil came increasingly to light. A decree of 1939, consolidating previous instructions, gave the police branch a definitive charter: in time of peace, as in time of war, to conduct counterespionage within the frontiers of France. Its functions are of two kinds: to obtain information about spies and to follow it up by the action necessary to bring them to justice. At first punishable by a maximum of five years imprisonment, the penalty in 1936 was twenty years, in 1938, death. The 1939 decree states that the Minister of the Interior is responsible for domestic counterespionage and that he has a specialized police, the *Surveillance du Territoire,* which is in no circumstances to be used for general police purposes in the maintenance of order.

During the 1930s the police counterespionage officers worked closely and fruitfully with the officers of the military *Deuxième Bureau.* The Army testimony is warm in praise of the sheer good will shown by the police in cooperating with them. Together they had to combat incredible apathy on the part of government and public alike towards national security. Progress was made, nevertheless: in 1937 there were 150 arrests of spies; in 1939, 400; in 1940, 1,000. With the German victory in 1940, France's counterespionage branches were disbanded under the terms of the Armistice.

They did not cease their activities. Under cover of Vichy staff appointments and commercial business, the Chief of the Army's secret services, Lieutenant-Colonel Louis Rivet, and his chief of counterespionage, Commandant Paillole, carried on their war against the German intelligence machine and the traitors who worked for it. In this task they had the covert help of the police and the Gendarmerie. Paul Paillole tells the story in his faultless memoirs, *Services Spéciaux (1935–1945)*, of how they kept alive the concept of treason in France and North Africa, did much damage to the Nazis and their agents, and supplied the Allies with invaluable intelligence.

Police in Uniform

FROM 1900 TO 1939

During the first four decades of the twentieth century the state of the civil police in the urban centers of provincial France left a great deal to be desired. Conditions of service for the personnel varied from place to place, local dignitaries exercised undesirable influence in police affairs, and the police themselves were ready and anxious for changes to improve their lot. Marcel Sicot tells the story of the Communist mayor of a small town who took pleasure in showing his cronies the miserable office he had allocated to "his" police chief, which he called "the cage where I've put my commissaire of police."

In theory, the Director of the *Sûreté* was in control of the commissaires, who were subject to inspection by the Controllers-General from Paris, but in practice the local authorities were more to be feared than any visiting functionary, however exalted in rank. The Controller-General might be here today (with luck, probably not) but the mayor and his "exec," the deputy mayor, would be here tomorrow.

The police of the city of Lyon had escaped from local municipal control when nationalized by Louis-Napoleon in 1851. During the early twentieth century Marseille, Toulon, and Nice were similarly released from mayoral bondage and put under the control of the respective departmental prefects.

The First World War drained the two police services, civil and military, of manpower. Four thousand civil police were recalled at once to their regiments and the Gendarmerie had to provide the provost police of France's newly mobilized armies. Hennion, now Prefect of Police, asked for five regiments of troops to help him to police Paris and was promptly dismissed. A further drain was the requirement for the police to provide men to staff a *Sûreté aux armées* (army security service), an investigative branch to be active in the pursuit of sedition, thus acquiring much odium. A dismal event was the prosecution for treason of the Minister of the Interior and the Director of the *Sûreté,* who had refrained from repressing defeatist propaganda from the Left, for fear, it was argued, of provoking a rising.

From 1914 to 1918 the police were under the ultimate control of the Minister of War. Clemenceau, "The Tiger," gave the police reinforcements from the Army in 1917 and saw to it that they were able to cope with the increasing incidence of public disorder and espionage. Crime presented, as so often in wartime, less than its usual difficulty: potential delinquents were preoccupied with fighting the Germans. On the whole, the consensus was that the police had acquitted themselves sensibly and well.

In the period between the two World Wars, the *Sûreté* had under its direct control less personnel than the Prefecture of Police of Paris. The police on central appointments, including those of the four cities whose forces had been nationalized, comprised some 1,400 commissaires, 1,000 plain-clothes officers, and a couple of thousand *gardiens de la paix.* The Paris police, with 14,000 *gardiens,* hundreds of plain-clothes *inspecteurs,* and 80 commissaires, was better staffed and very much better trained. The *Sûreté's* commissaires certainly envied their Parisian counterparts, who could count on a fixed residence for the whole of their career, whereas they could be transferred at any time to any urban center in France. Such transfers could be made arbitrarily, for disciplinary reasons or when some hapless commissaire had aroused the dislike of a local bigwig.

In the 1930s, the relative importance of the *Sûreté* and the Prefecture of Police, both with their headquarters in central Paris, the one at the Ministry of the Interior in the rue des Saussaies, the other on the Ile de la Cité, was much canvassed. Willy-Paul Romain, in his *Dossiers de la Police,* quotes a report from the Minister of the Interior to the president of the Republic on April 28,

1934, seeking to acquire for the *Sûreté* a status equal to that of the Prefecture of Police:

> The *Sûreté Nationale* is no longer the poor relation, with its director, its four departments and its two judicial and administrative controls. It is a great establishment whose chiefs, once placed on an equal footing with their colleagues of the Prefecture of Police, will naturally maintain cordial relations which hardly exist except between officials of the same rank.

But parity did not exist. The Prefect of Police, whose post dated back to Napoleon I, had a status considerably higher than that of the Director of the *Sûreté*. Even in the 1960s, it was regarded as a promotion for the Director of the *Sûrete* to be appointed Prefect of Police of Paris. The two great establishments for many years to come would differ even to the point of each having its own political bias, the *Sûreté* to the Left, the Prefecture of Police to the Right. "Cordial relations" between two very distinct police organizations, each jealously maintaining its own system of criminal records, whose activities inevitably encroached upon one another's, did not exist, though there were outstanding instances of cooperation between individuals.

The Gendarmerie had organized its capacity to deal with public turbulence by making available in each department a company for this purpose. In 1921 these companies were reinforced by the formation of eighty-seven platoons to specialize in the maintenance of public order. It was from these bodies that the modern Gendarmerie Mobile was formed in 1954.

The February Riots of 1934

The Paris riots of February 1934 were the worst outbreaks of public violence that France had seen since the carnage of the Commune in 1871. They provide a classic case study of "high police" and of the maintenance of public order.

France between the World Wars was in a continuous state of internal conflict. The 1914–1918 war had cost her 1,400,000 killed and left her a long legacy of permanently maimed men and bereaved families. The Bolshevik Revolution in Russia had

81

divided the labor movement, alienating from the Third Republic those who saw their salvation in international Communism, while economic woes alienated the rest of the organized working class. The rise of Fascism in Italy and Germany encouraged those of the extreme Right, the believers in the black shirt and the brown shirt as the panacea against the hammer and sickle, and the royalists, who had never accepted republicanism, to move to a new and dangerous level of antagonism to the Third Republic. Here was the divided France again, the France Fouché had been able to keep in equilibrium, but there was no Fouché among the mediocre politicians of the time, and if there had been he would have accomplished little without another Napoleon to distract the nation from internal discord by the suspense, the spoils, and the glory of victorious wars in other lands.

In the sphere of "high police" there was a disastrous lack of realism. This is hardly to be wondered at, for between 1920 and 1934 the successive governments had averaged about six months in office. This instability at the highest level of administration hopelessly handicapped the men who were especially responsible for coping with the dangers to the state: the prime minister, the Minister of the Interior, the Minister of Justice, and the Minister of War.

One unmistakable sign of the degeneration of governmental control was the incidence of large-scale financial crime, and it was a swindle of considerable magnitude that precipitated the 1934 riots.

The frauds of Sacha Stavisky, an impressive entrepreneur who was cutting quite a figure in fashionable society by gambling hugely in the casinos and spending other people's money in other spectacular ways, had been known for some time to the police. The police had reported them—in vain. Their senior officers would not move against him. The public prosecutors proved equally unhelpful. At the Prefecture of Police and at the *Sûreté Nationale* the misdeeds of Stavisky had been signaled to the highest level. Nothing was done. The fact that the two headquarters did not communicate their data to each other did not help.

Whether fear of provoking a financial catastrophe that might result in unforeseeable mischief was the reason, or whether corruption within their organizations was to blame—both on the face of it seem highly likely—the police and judicial authorities deferred action until the extremist newspapers learned that the collapse of Stavisky's baseless financial empire was imminent. The most virulent articles appeared, castigating both the government and the police. Vainly, the prime minister promised reform. Stavisky fled to Chamonix. The police at last were ordered to arrest him. Before they could do so, he committed suicide.

The hostile press found this incredible. It was too convenient for the authorities. They published wild and totally unjustified statements that the swindler had been murdered by the police.

The government was defeated and fell. A new administration was formed under Edouard Daladier, with Frot as Minister of the Interior. They resolved on the bold step of getting rid of the Prefect of Police, Jean Chiappe. This they proposed to do by giving him higher office as Resident-General in Morocco.

Chiappe was a stylish and independent Prefect of Police. He had done good things, providing welfare facilities for the service beginning a one-way street system and installing traffic lights, bringing women into the Prefecture of Police as "assistants" to do worthwhile work, improving police communications and the delivery of services. He was immensely popular with his *gardiens de la paix.* Exceptionally experienced, he had been Director of the *Sûreté* for three years and Prefect of Police for seven. The Prefecture had become his satrapy, "a state within the State." When Daladier offered him the Moroccan Residency-General he categorically refused it and said he would stay where he was. Daladier had no viable alternative; on February 3, 1934, he dismissed him from his post.

This caused a great stir. The Socialist papers were in favor of the dismissal, believing (with more than a little justice) that Chiappe had been tougher on their demonstrations than those of their bitter enemies on the Right. The extreme Right's journals and speakers raised a fearsome outcry against the victimization of one of their heroes. The Right organizations on which they could call for public protest were formidable in numbers and in preparedness to make trouble. The call went out for mass demonstrations on Tuesday, February 6, 1934.

A new Prefect of Police, Adrien Bonnefoy-Sibour, until then

Prefect of the Department of Seine-et-Oise, was hastily installed. The police contingency plan, dating according to Marcel Le Clère (whose book, *Le 6 février,* is the great authority on the subject), as far back as 1919, was brought out of the files as the blueprint for the police operations. The General Intelligence branch of the Prefecture sent in its forecast of what was to be expected: a crowd of at least ten thousand, half of whom, being ex-soldiers, could be relied upon to behave decently. The rallying point would be the Grand-Palais. On this report the Prefect of Police and his operations staff founded their dispositions. General Intelligence then sent in a second forecast, to the effect that the Place de la Concorde would see a hostile crowd of several thousand between 8.00 and 9:00 P.M. This report never reached its destination, having been sidetracked into some bureaucratic impasse, and came to light only after the emergency was over.

The new Prefect soon ran into trouble. The Director-General of the Municipal Police, Paul Guichard, immensely experienced in order maintenance, a firm friend of Chiappe, went down with appendicitis on February 5th. His second-in-command, Camille Marchand, thus became the Prefect's operational commander. They counted heads: they could put out 3,800 *gardiens de la paix,* 2,200 gendarmes of the Republican Guard. General Intelligence warned that this might be too few. The Prefect decided to ask for fifteen platoons (each of twenty-five men) from the Gendarmerie Mobile. Three companies of firemen were also detailed.

The likeliest objective, it was thought, would be the Elysée Palace, residence of the president of the Republic. Others highly probable were the Hotel de Ville, headquarters of the municipal government, a classical revolutionary target since 1789, and the Chamber of Deputies, the lower house of the legislature, the seat of which was the Palais Bourbon, reached by a bridge over the River Seine from the Place de la Concorde. This last was a great public space, with several streets leading out of it and bordered by gardens and trees.

In the event, the forces of order had to face three times the number of demonstrators they had been led to expect, and the prinicipal objective, the one for which least defense had been provided, turned out to be the Palais Bourbon. Though action raged along the boulevards of central Paris and the other foreseen objectives were seriously threatened, the major confrontation was in the Place de la Concorde, where the demonstrators continually sought to force the passage of the bridge over the Seine and impose their presence on the legislators.

From about 4.00 P.M. they began to group in the Place de la Concorde. By 4.45 P.M. the defenses of the bridge were in place: a commissaire of police, four subordinate officers, seventy *gardiens de la paix*, one hundred gendarmes on foot, and twenty-five cavalrymen of the Republican Guard. There were no rifles for the military police, in pursuance of the policy of not threatening the public with arms. The only firearms were the individual sidearms of the police and the gendarmes. Seven police buses were parked side by side on the bridge, radiators facing the Palais Bourbon, to form a barricade. Fire hoses were in place. The Prefect of Police and his field commander, Marchand, with the General Intelligence chief, Perrier, established a command post between the bridge and the Chamber of Deputies.

Pressure built up as successive columns of demonstrators marched into the place de la Concorde. In front of the police barricade the shouting started, execrating the government, exalting the dismissed Chiappe, and appealing to the police to join the demonstration. The Guard cavalry went out, trotting, sabers sheathed, to clear the approaches of the bridge. They were received with a hail of chunks of paving stones, pieces of iron grating torn up from round the trees in the gardens, and impacted balls of coal dust on which the horses lost their footing. Later the horses would have to face razor slashing and sand flung in their eyes. The commissaire on the bridge called for reinforcements.

The demonstrators, beyond the defenders' reach, were building their own barricades as a strong point to the left of the bridge. The gas lamps, smashed, provided minor furnaces in which to heat their iron missiles, fearsome ammunition against men who had no riot gear. The first reinforcements arrived at 6.30 P.M., in the form of Colonel Simon, of the Republican Guard, and 175 gendarmes.

By now the demonstrators were almost up to the barricade on the bridge. Police casualties were mounting fast: most of the cavalry had been struck by missiles and there were many head injuries among the men on foot. At 7.00 P.M. Marchand decided it was high time to issue the statutory warning to the attackers: "We are going to use force." The demonstrators were unimpressed. Marchand, who had stood on the parapet of the bridge with a Guard trumpeter to blow for attention, was hit in the face by a piece of stone and the soldier was badly hurt. A little sporadic firing came from the crowd after the cavalry had gone out again and been driven back. A gendarme was wounded.

The pressure on the police barricade intensified. There was a moment of panic and the defenders began to fall back. Rallied by a lieutenant of the Guard, the gendarmes dropped to one knee and began to fire individually, though no order to fire had been given. This had the effect of making the crowd recoil, but people were killed and wounded. Police were firing over the heads of the rioters—a practice that was strictly forbidden. Marchand shouted for them to holster their guns.

Elsewhere in central Paris there were barricades and hand-to-hand fighting. The Ministry of Marine was set on fire. Weber's restaurant in the rue Royale was being used as a field hospital. In the Place de la Concorde the veterans were marching, blind and crippled men and decorated ex-officers much in evidence. The police and military strength was rapidly draining away in casualties.

Across the field of fire between the rioters and the barricade missiles were being hurled, with the police throwing them back at their assailants, always a bad sign. The fire hoses drenched as many defenders as attackers. Responding to shots fired by the rioters, some police and gendarmes again opened unauthorized fire. More people fell.

Colonel Simon lost patience twenty minutes before midnight. He ordered his gendarmes to charge, leading them himself, and cleared all before him. A parallel and equally spirited drive by the police, unfortunately accompanied by more unauthorized fire, causing casualties, cleared the other side of the square. By midnight the Place de la Concorde, littered with debris, smashed kiosks, overturned vehicles, luridly illuminated by streaming blue flares from broken gas mains, was empty.

Casualties, the full extent of which, as always on such occasions, is unknown because many are never reported, were heavy indeed. With the lesser but still formidable riots that the forces of order had to overcome on the following day, the February riots cost over 30 lives, nearly 400 admissions to hospital, and over 1,500 wounds were dressed.

The extreme Right had sought the overthrow of the Republic, in vain, but if the regime was saved, the government was not. Daladier had to go. A "national" government under a former president of the Republic was formed to replace his administration. A month later the Prefect of Police was replaced.

It is unfair to blame Bonnefoy-Sibour, who was Prefect of Police for only three days at the time of the debacle. He stood at his post throughout, sensibly leaving the operational command to the professional officers, though he erred early in the confrontation when he prevented Marchand from having the gardens beside the square cleared; that was where the iron missiles were obtained.

The command deficiencies were many. The contingency plan had not been updated. Intelligence had been faulty, its communication worse. The General Intelligence branch's grasp of the extremist parties' intentions and resources was weak and its presentation of the syntheses of its information to the authorities seems to have been lacking in the necessary emphasis. The coordination of the defense elements was much at fault. There had been virtually no prior consultation with the Gendarmerie. Some of the legal procedures for requisitioning military aid had not been followed, resulting in the nonappearance of expected reinforcements. The Prefect of Police apparently did not know what forces he had in reserve because no one reported their arrival to him. The responsibility for command in the front line was divided and confusing. The police and gendarmes were deployed in mixed units; each was uncertain about which officer's orders they should obey. The principle of close-knit, homogeneous units, strongly officered and stiffened by NCOs was not observed. There was criticism of the use of cavalry on the slippery surfaces of central Paris against rioters adept in combating it, but over the years mounted police have proved their worth in riot situations all over the world.

Equipment was deficient. There were no steel helmets for the police, which led to many injuries that would have been prevented by their use. There was no material for police barricades save what could be improvised on the spot. Communications were scanty—a single telephone line to the command post of such a large-scale operation. With hindsight, it seems wrong that the gendarmes were not issued with rifles or carbines. The mere sight of a hedge of leveled barrels is a powerful deterrent and the rifle butt is a handy weapon at close quarters. But who knows what the soldiers' reaction might have been if they had been ordered to prepare to fire on their fellow citizens, many of whom, on this particular occasion, had fought beside them against the Germans in the First World War?

One might conclude that the forces of order finally secured the upper hand because, as is not infrequently the case in similar emergencies, a lot of men did their best. But many failed to report for duty, others opened fire without orders, and it is possible that at least at the outset of the operation the force's regard for Chiappe and their resentment of the apparently idiotic manner of his dismissal (why promote him to a much higher post if he was an unsatisfactory Prefect of Police?) made them less than eager to do their duty, though in the heat of the conflict the necessary determination asserted itself.

In the longer view, the whole affair, from the depredations of Stavisky to the long lines of casualties in the hospitals, must be blamed on a political regime that gave none of its leaders a chance to see its problems steadily and to see them whole. There at the ultimate point of "high police" the real failure lay.

THE SECOND WORLD WAR

The Second World War, bringing at first partial and then total occupation by the enemy, was particularly hard on the police. What should a police officer do in such a situation? It is one that American and British police have never had to face.

Several courses were open to the French police during the period 1940–1944. One was to collaborate with the enemy, a course some took. Like many of their fellow countrymen (and many in other countries, too), they may have thought that it was better for the Nazis to win the war (which in 1940–1941 they certainly looked like doing) than for Europe to be overrun by Russian Communism: a nice choice, between Hitler and Stalin, the two great butchers of all time. Resignation was another course, taken by some, but if very many officers had opted out, the policing of their fellow citizens (and themselves) would have been in the heavy hands of the German *feldgendarmerie*. To stay on the job, to carry on as best they could with the protection of the community and the repression of crime, was the third alternative, which most police chose. A fourth alternative, often a corollary to the third, lay in the activities of that many-headed movement, the Resistance, in which a great many civil police and gendarmes involved themselves.

As Marcel Le Clère and Henry Buisson have recorded in their respective histories of the police, the Germans were not long in realizing that the obstruction they came up against, the delays in carrying out their orders, were calculated to minimize their efficacy. Reprisals were swift. A Prefect of Police was arrested, as were many commissaires of the Paris force, which had 154 killed as well as many who died on active service with the armed forces. The *Sûreté Nationale* lost 373 by execution or in the Liberation fighting, 35 who died from torture, 1,048 deported, 315 of whom died. The Gendarmerie lost 338 killed or executed, 154 killed in Resistance operations, 1,319 deported, 258 of whom died. The Vichy Government also inflicted many thousands of punishments, including imprisonment, on the civil police and Gendarmerie alike. Thus, there is ample statistical evidence that the fourth alternative was the one most favored by the police services. There were also strong undercover police networks fighting the secret war against the occupying power.

Despite the adverse forces with which the police had to contend, their organizational development continued to make valuable progress. The winds of Vichy, ill as they were, nevertheless blew some good that survived the Liberation and became incorporated in the modern police system.

Since before the outbreak of war in 1939, the *Sûreté's* professional organizations had been pressing for their conditions of service to be standardized, which entailed the nationalization of the police forces of the municipalities. The Vichy Government, more concerned with getting control of the police than with improving conditions, proceeded in 1941 to lay hands on the majority of the provincial police by nationalizing the forces of all municipalities with ten thousand or more inhabitants. That, at least, was the intention, but municipally recruited forces under mayoral control have never entirely disappeared. The nationalization of the police of communes of ten thousand or more population went on slowly and a quarter of a century later had not been fully implemented. A great step towards centralization of the civil police system had nevertheless been taken and there was to be no regression from it.

Vichy's other positive contribution to police development was the establishment of a higher training college for the *Sûreté*. The *Ecole Nationale Supérieure de Police* (usually known in Britain and the United States as "the French Police College") was founded in 1941 at Saint-Cyr-au-Mont-d'Or, a few miles from Lyon. Its function was to train aspirants to the rank of commissaire of police. The Germans kept an eye on it; the Deputy Director and two members of the faculty were arrested and deported.

In 1941 the Vichy Government also formed Reserve Groups of civil police, some 19,000 strong, for the maintenance of order. The Mobile Gendarmerie was abolished during the Occupation and this formation was designed to take its place.

In any general consideration of police during those years must be mentioned the sinister parallel police established by Vichy in 1943, the *Milice* (Militia). The militia soon broke away from the purpose for which the government had intended it and became a Fascist political police in close cooperation with the SS. Its leader, Joseph Darnand, had the title of Secretary-General for the Maintenance of Order; in 1944 he became Secretary of State for the Interior. The militia were the Resistance's worst enemies.

The regular police and the Gendarmerie usually managed to lend a helping hand to the Resistance in its multifarious operations. There was much they could do, and did, often at the cost of their own lives and liberties: warning people on whom the Gestapo was about to descend, fabricating identity cards, facilitating the escape of Allied airmen, making false returns, covering parachute drops and Allied take-offs and landings, complicating and impeding the German-ordained measures of the government.

The men of the Prefecture of Police made a cardinal contribution to the Liberation of Paris. They refused duty, seized the Prefecture buildings, and fought the German garrison. Their casualties were heavy on this occasion: 150 killed. It was altogether fitting that it was to the Prefecture of Police that the

Wehrmacht commander, General von Choltitz, came on August 25, 1944, to sign the instrument of capitulation.

With the Liberation came a dreadful reckoning. There was a massive purge of the police as old scores and grudges were paid off and denunciations of "collaboration" poured indiscriminately forth. The spirit of revenge, which Francis Bacon defined as "a kind of wild justice," was prevalent. Wild indeed was the "justice" that caused some seven thousand police to be dismissed. In Paris alone five commissaires were executed and fifty-four deprived of office.

REPUBLICAN SECURITY COMPANIES

In 1944 the Gendarmerie was heavily engaged in its military role with the armies fighting the last year of the war with the Nazis. The government, faced with endless post-Occupation conflict and disorder, felt the need of a reserve force that could be deployed to preserve or restore public order. The model of the Mobile Reserve Groups (which had vanished with the Liberation) was adopted and in 1945 the *Compagnies républicaines de sécurité* were formed. A decree in 1948 defined them as "mobile police units placed under the authority of the Minister of the Interior."

The style of these Republican Security Companies, generally known as the CRS, is so much a military one that it is necessary to emphasize that all their personnel are civil police officers. Sixty-one companies, formed into ten groups, are stationed in their own barracks, situated whence they can best be deployed, all over France. Each company is self-sufficient in transportation and equipment and can move fast at short notice to the scene of trouble. The total strength is approximately 16,000 men, nearly equal to the present strength of the Mobile Gendarmerie. The discipline is military.

So, as the Second World War came to its end, the central government of France had very considerably tightened its hold upon an augmented police. The nationalization of every sizeable police force, the creation of the national police academy, the bringing into being of a massive new striking force: these measures mark a crucial stage in the centralization of the police system.

CHAPTER 7

Police Development Since 1945

New Republics

The purge of the police mentioned in the previous chapter was only a small part of the Liberation's "wild justice." Death sentences by the courts rose to over two thousand, of which some seven hundred were carried out. Forty thousand prison sentences were handed down. The number of those killed by extralegal action, the number of other sanctions, will never be known. The legacy of recrimination has not yet been spent.

The Fourth Republic came into being in November 1946, amid a general lack of enthusiasm which its record would more than vindicate. Over twenty governments came and went before 1958, with unsavory political intrigues generating the aura of immorality that had so often surrounded the Third Republic's conduct of the nation's affairs. Indo-China, Tunisia, Morocco were lost, Algeria in a ferment. Economically, the ravages of the Occupation and the devastation caused by the Allied bombardments and invasion, and the subsequent fighting on French soil had left an enormous task of reconstruction, while Communist-fomented strikes retarded industrial recovery and disturbed public order.

Algeria, most highly prized of all France's colonies, where a million white settlers, most of whose families had been established there for generations, were determined to remain under French sovereignty, was torn by guerrilla war waged by the Muslims, who were equally determined to achieve independence. France had to maintain half a million troops there and to reinforce the police with substantial drafts from the mainland. Many of the troops had been embittered by the defeat at Dien-Bien-Phu, and the army and the white settlers became increasingly rebellious to the Fourth Republic's government in Paris.

On May 13, 1958, the settlers, unopposed by the army, seized the government buildings in Algiers. In Paris there was great disaffection, not least among the police. It seemed possible, in this month of crisis, that the paratroopers might fly from North Africa and descend on the capital. At this juncture, General de Gaulle was recalled to form a new government. On January 1, 1959, the Fifth Republic began.

The work of national reconstruction was carried on strongly, and would restore France to economic health, but the magnitude of the Algerian dilemma dwarfed all other problems during the early years of the new Republic. From early 1955 the Muslim revolt's spearhead, the FLN (National Liberation Front) had been mounting increasingly intense guerrilla war. Its terrorist arm was now carrying out assassinations in metropolitan France as well as in North Africa. The government was also being harassed by an underground French resistance group, the OAS (Secret Army Organization), recruited from settlers, ex-soldiers, soldiers who were not "ex," and rightist foes of the Republic. The OAS would never forgive de Gaulle for recognizing Algeria's independence in July 1962, charging that the man whom the settlers and the army had swept into power in 1958 in the belief that he would secure France's interests in North Africa had betrayed their trust. They went on trying to kill him until 1966.

The burden borne by the police during those years was a heavy one. They had to cope with two powerful terrorist organizations at once, while ordinary crime was well into its postwar escalation. Many police officers had been killed on duty during the past three years and the government was dragging its feet interminably over a pay rise when, on March 13, 1958, three thousand police bar-

93

racked the Prefect and marched in protest to the Palais Bourbon to bring their grievances to the legislators' notice. The resolution of the Algerian struggle in 1962 brought considerable relief and enabled the police to redress the balance of their efforts.

In the postwar reconstruction of the police system, the counterespionage branch, the *Surveillance du Territoire,* acquired a status very different from that of the prewar years. The branch had then enjoyed little initiative, being regarded as the means whereby the *Deuxième Bureau* of the armed forces and the public prosecutors could have inquiries and arrests made. The reform of police counterespionage was chiefly the work of one man: Wybot.

The story began in 1941, when a young and very able artillery captain, Roger Warin, who had been engaged in the secret struggle in German-occupied France, escaped to London to join the Free French Forces there. He was promptly employed in their intelligence organization; he worked for a year directing the counterespionage section where his knowledge of the Resistance networks in France proved invaluable. It was at this time that he took the pseudonym "Wybot," by which he has continued to be known. It was the practice for Free French soldiers to disguise their identity for fear of reprisals against their families at home. Wybot's outspoken, professional, and uncompromising attitude, however, incurred the displeasure of General de Gaulle, and he chose to go out to fight with line units in North Africa and Italy.

When Liberation came, he made his way to Paris. The Minister of the Interior appointed him to assist in the reorganization of the *Sûreté Nationale.* His counterespionage and Resistance record, despite his lack of regular police experience, led to his being placed in charge of the DST, which was then being rather awkwardly reconstituted after its years of suspension during the Occupation.

Wybot was determined, in his dedicated and intransigent way, to recast and reorient the service. This led to near-mutiny and much intrigue on the part of the returning officers of the former dispensation but he was not to be intimidated and soon made himself master in his own house. Taking the classical view that secret services are always at war, he directed the DST at a heightened tempo, installing a crucial documentation section and new technological means of surveillance, insisting on meticulous paperwork and systematic interrogation, demanding of his officers a quality of work that they eventually were proud to achieve. Instead of waiting for leads from the military, the DST, revitalized, now took the initiative.

Wybot directed police counterespionage for fifteen years, untamed by politicians and administrative dignitaries, and despite the obstructions caused by the rivalry of the *Sûreté* and the Prefecture of Police. The government conceded him the status of a Director, giving the service a further degree of independence. When de Gaulle came to power in 1958 he lost little time in relegating Wybot to other duties, but the DST's new place in the police structure survived his removal.

Scandal and Reorganization

THE BEN BARKA AFFAIR*

Agomehdia Ben Barka was a leader of the political opposition in France's former protectorate, Morocco. He had been condemned to death in absentia after he had fled from the fury of the right-wing government of his country and was living in Egypt. General Oufkir, Moroccan Minister of the Interior, resolved to put an end to him. Oufkir had been an officer in the French Army prior to French tutelage being lifted in 1956 and is reported to have held a senior appointment in those days in the French secret service, the SDECE (*Service de Documentation extérieure et de Contre-espionage:* Foreign Documentation and Counter-Espionage Service), the functions of which are to seek intelligence in foreign countries and foil espionage beyond France's frontiers, the domestic field being the DST's preserve.

In order to lure Ben Barka from his Cairo asylum, General Oufkir and his intelligence service formed a plot that required a great deal of French participation. The link-man was to be Antoine Lopez, a man of many parts: ostensibly an airline inspector at Orly Airport, he was working, too, in a dual capacity as an informant

---

* The clearest press account of the Ben Barka affair I have found is the "Insight" article in the London *Sunday Times* of January 23, 1966.

both for the SDECE and the Prefecture of Police's narcotics squad. He was also an agent of the Moroccan secret service.

Lopez recruited conspirators. He found Philippe Bernier, who had been negotiating with the hapless Ben Barka about making a documentary film. A "backer" for the film was now named, the part being played by an ex-convict, Georges Figon, and four or five other unsavory characters were brought into the enterprise. A mere gangster coup was out of the question: big money, a million francs, was being mentioned, and other profits might be expected to accrue; the affair had to have some official color if Ben Barka was to be effectively snared. Lopez had the answer. He used his relationship with the Paris drugs squad to involve its commissaire and his second-in-command, by giving them to understand that the operation was being mounted by the SDECE.

The stratagem worked. Ben Barka, with a companion, flew to Paris. At the airport he was received by the Prefecture of Police officer who routinely saw Moroccan personages and then went on his way to an appointment with the film makers, set for 12.30 P.M., October 29, 1965, on the boulevard Saint-Germain. The officer who had seen him at the airport was keeping an eye on him and had taken a seat on the other side of the carriageway. Ben Barka was looking in a shop window when the drugs squad commissaire and his aide appeared. They produced their official identification and asked him, but not his companion, to accompany them. He was ushered to a police car, in which the two officers, Lopez, and one of the gang drove off with him. The other members of the gang, on the sidewalk, stood so as to prevent Ben Barka's friend seeing the registration plates. The surveillance officer, across the boulevard, recognized police colleagues and assumed that all was well. The conspirators, however, had taken a fatal risk, counting on the incident being unreported. But the surveillance officer had noted down the number of the car.

That was the last to be seen of Ben Barka. It would appear that General Oufkir, in France at that time, had him killed somewhere in the suburbs and caused the body to be hidden. Oufkir flew home two days later.

The Prefecture of Police's observer reported the occurrence in the Boulevard Saint-Germain. The General Intelligence branch investigated and informed the Criminal Intelligence branch. A report went to the Prefect of Police. The Minister of the Interior was informed, and President de Gaulle was given a much-edited account of the matter. The case was given for investigation to the chief of the Prefecture of Police's élite detective squad, the *brigade criminelle*. Action swiftly followed. Lopez was arrested, his two police contacts were suspended, and the gangsters began to run. Georges Figon began to talk to the press, seeking to cover himself. The police organized a large-scale hunt for him but when they found him he was dead, apparently having committed suicide, though less convincingly than Stavisky.

Now the publicity raged, condemning the secret service and the police, and accusing de Gaulle of having hushed up the whole business until he had won the presidential election. A rally of ten thousand opponents of the government, through their spokesman, François Mitterand, called on the General to resign.

The General did not resign. He decided to reorganize the police.

CONSOLIDATION: THE POLICE NATIONALE

On the afternoon of Tuesday, June 21, 1966, the Chamber of Deputies was sitting in the Palais Bourbon. The business, a government proposal to reorganize the civil police, had been formally declared "urgent" and the legislators were having their say. The Communist Party's spokesman did not mince his words:

Ladies and gentlemen, the reform of the police is an ancient and important problem. But if it is tackled today by the National Assembly, it is to the dramatic spin-off from the Ben Barka affair that this is due.

One recalls, indeed, the stupefaction of French public opinion when it learned that the criminal abduction, in the middle of Paris, of the leader of the Moroccan Opposition, had been the result of the joint action, long prepared, of authentic policemen, crooks, occasional collaborators of the police, agents of the S.D.E.C.E. and men from foreign secret services operating freely on our territory.*

The Communist deputies, he said, did not think that the present measure would reassure the public in the least.

*Le Journal Officiel de la République Française. Débats Parlementaires. Assemblée Nationale. Mercredi 22 juin 1966.

The Minister of the Interior rose to justify the government's proposal. The reforms envisaged had often been contemplated in the past. It was a question of the *duality* of the police system:

> Indeed, until now, the Prefecture of Police was a veritable central administration with its own territorial jurisdiction, depending directly on the Minister of the Interior, the governance of which was handled—for, you will recall, a municipal administration was involved—by the Ministry of the Interior's general control of local services. The relationship between the general direction of the *Sûreté Nationale* and the Prefecture of Police could only function through the intermediary of the Minister himself or, on occasion, of his cabinet.
>
> From now on, it will be appropriate to install, near to the Minister, a unified administration, the jurisdiction of which will extend over the whole country and over all services with limited territorial jurisdiction, including the Prefecture of Police.
>
> What will be the role of such an administration? It must have an overall view of the activity of all the services, apportion resources in matériel and personnel, supervise recruitment, training and discipline of such personnel, compile the texts whereby the regulation-making power of the Minister of the Interior is exercised and prepare the directives he issues.
>
> More particularly it will have to control and animate the services directly attached to the Ministry, whether they have national jurisdiction or regional jurisdiction, like the units of the Counter-Espionage Service or the regional crime services, with the reservation, in the latter case, of the exclusive attributions of the judicial authorities.
>
> A precise example will allow the new structure to be better understood: the central directorates of the police's operational services will henceforth be able to give instructions to the directorates of the Prefecture of Police, just as they do, and will continue to do, in the case of the regional services; the sole difference will be that these instructions will necessarily be given through the Prefect of Police.
>
> The General Intelligence services will henceforth constitute a homogeneous network over the whole country, which will enable the government to have, in all spheres concerning governmental action, a view at once more general and more complete of political, economic and social realities.[*]

The proposal, little modified in debate, became law on July 9,

[*]Ibid.

1966. It established the Police Nationale, under the authority of the Minister of the Interior, of which all police, whether of the *Sûreté* or the Prefecture of Police, would be members.

The head of the new administration at the Ministry was to be the Secretary-General of the Police Nationale; in 1969 this post was abolished and replaced by that of the Director-General of the Police Nationale. Since that date, the *Sûreté Nationale* has ceased to exist, its personnel being consolidated in the Police Nationale. The Prefecture of Police, though its personnel and matériel are provided under the Director-General's arrangements, continues to enjoy operational independence under its own Prefect.

Big changes, nevertheless, were inevitable for the Paris force. In 1964, the Department of the Seine, classical jurisdiction of the Prefect of Police of Paris, was divided into four administrative areas. These are the City of Paris, and the three Departments of Hauts-de-Seine, Seine-Saint-Denis, and Val de Marne. For the period needed to implement the change, the Prefect of Police remained responsible for police services in all four areas and it was not until 1971 that the prefects of the three new departments were given the same police responsibilities as the prefects of the provincial departments. In each of the three departments, however, were two detective services, part of the Prefecture of Police's criminal investigation network, supplementing the departmental detective services in the same manner as the regional police services in the provinces supplement the detective resources of the urban centers.

The jurisdiction of the Prefect of Police was thus severely curtailed. From 1971 the population he polices was reduced from approximately six and a half to two and a half million.

The minister's speech to the Chamber of Deputies, quoted above, made much of the benefits to be expected from a unified General Intelligence service. Until then the daily synthesis of the Prefecture of Police's information had been presented each evening to the minister by the Prefect. As the most significant items of the whole national picture were usually to do with Paris, this gave a particular importance to the Prefect of Police in his relations with the government. Now the Prefecture's information would pass to the central directorate of General Intelligence where the national synthesis was prepared and presented to the

THE POLICE NATIONALE

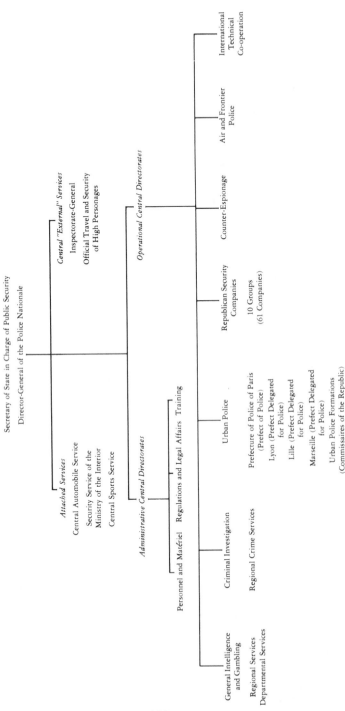

Minister of the Interior and of Decentralization

Secretary of State in Charge of Public Security

Director-General of the Police Nationale

Attached Services
Central Automobile Service
Security Service of the Ministry of the Interior
Central Sports Service

Central "External" Services
Inspectorate-General
Official Travel and Security of High Personages

Administrative Central Directorates

Personnel and Matériel   Regulations and Legal Affairs   Training

Criminal Investigation

Regional Crime Services

Urban Police

Prefecture of Police of Paris (Prefect of Police)
Lyon (Prefect Delegated for Police)
Lille (Prefect Delegated for Police)
Marseille (Prefect Delegated for Police)
Urban Police Formations (Commissaires of the Republic)

General Intelligence and Gambling

Regional Services
Departmental Services

Operational Central Directorates

Republican Security Companies

10 Groups (61 Companies)

Counter-Espionage

Air and Frontier Police

International Technical Co-operation

2.

minister. Thus, from being the bearer of potentially momentous tidings, the Prefect became the recipient of a copy of what had been presented by the central directorate.

The Prefecture of Police's legendary criminal investigation branch after 1971 became classed as one more regional crime service. As it is by far the largest of them, with its 3,200 police officers, some account of it may help to make the position clear.

The branch's activities are coordinated by its headquarters at 36, quai des Orfèvres. Here there are three operational divisions. The most important of these is the *Sous-Direction des Affaires Criminelles* (Sub-Directorate of Criminal Affairs) which groups five squads dealing with flagrant offenses and important inquiries. The *Brigade Criminelle,* the élite detective unit that Georges Simenon has made world-famous through his detective character Maigret, deals with grave offenses against the person or against property, in 1981 making 164 arrests, 97 of which led to prison sentences. The *Brigade de Recherches et d'Intervention* (Investigation and Intervention Squad), nicknamed the Anti-Gang Squad, seeks out persons likely to commit serious gang-style crimes in the course of its double task of providing criminal intelligence and catching criminals. The *Brigade de Répression du Banditisme* (Banditry Repression Squad) deals with aggravated breaking offenses, armed robbery, and such specialized crimes as pickpocketing and art forgery. In 1981 the squad tackled 773 offenses, 657 of them being cleared by arrest and 662 prison sentences were handed down. The *Brigade des Stupéfiants et du Proxnétisme* (Narcotics and Procuring—pimping—Squad) has two sections, one concerned with traffic in dangerous drugs and the other with the offenses of living off prostitution and trafficking in pornography. In 1981 the squad's activities resulted in 2,179 prison sentences. The *Brigade de Protection des Mineurs* (Juvenile Protection Squad) deals with offenses committed by or against minors, missing children, and endangerment of the young, in liaison with the social services and the juvenile courts. It runs a "welcome" bureau in the avenue Victoria for young foreign and French visitors to Paris. In 1981 the squad found proof of 334 offenses, resulting in 103 prison sentences.

The work of these specialist headquarters squads is complemented throughout Paris and the three peripheral departments by twelve *Brigades Territoriales* (Local Squads), six for Paris and, as previously noted, two for each of the departments. Each squad consists of forty to fifty officers, working in close touch with the neighboring commissariats of police. In 1981 their results included 7,867 offenses cleared, including 47 homicides, 134 armed robberies, 1,343 burglaries, 1,610 thefts from vehicles, 98 rapes, 219 living off prostitutes' earnings, 224 cases of illicit arms possession. Prison sentences numbered 7,065.

Among this important division's major resources are the Prefecture of Police's crime laboratory and its fingerprint and anthropometric department, the latter housing the Police Nationale's fingerprint collection.

The second subdirectorate is for Economic and Financial Affairs, where police officers work on behalf of the public prosecutors and *juges d'instruction* in such fields as fraud, forgery, swindling, infractions of the health laws and the laws on the press, check offenses, and infractions of labor and construction laws.

The third subdirectorate, General Services and Commissariats, is designed to work with Paris's fifty-one police commissariats and her three police centers, which constitute (among much else) the first line of criminal policing. It is to the neighborhood commissariat that crime is most usually reported and the local commissaire and local officers are usually first at the crime scene; their initial action can make or mar the success of an investigation. In 1981, 275,811 offenses were dealt with at commissariat level, with 28,300 persons apprehended and 5,797 prison sentences resulting.

If the Prefecture of Police's famous detective branch is now "only" another regional service, it is as well to bear in mind the volume of its business and the extent of its resources.*

It is hard, when considering the Prefecture of Police since the reforms of the 1960s, not to feel that the government has sought to diminish the power of the Prefect of Police. The reduction of territorial jurisdiction has gone hand in hand with the imposition of additional duties, since the Prefect is now also Prefect of the Paris Defense Zone. His General Intelligence and Criminal Inves-

---

*The foregoing account is based on the article "La Police Judiciaire" in *Liaisons*, no. 257 (mars–avril 1982).

tigation services have been made parts of a larger system and his past independence has been much reduced by subordination to the Director-General of the Police Nationale. The bold self-sufficiency of certain Prefects of Police in times gone by has no doubt been a factor in this development.

THE MAY RIOTS OF 1968

The public-order emergency of May–June 1968 was the most violent since the February Riots of 1934 and the most protracted since the Paris Commune in 1871. It very nearly brought down General de Gaulle's government, the fall of which would almost certainly have spelt the end of the Fifth Republic. The general himself nearly lost heart at one point. He admitted that on May 29th he was tempted to withdraw, but, "I thought that if I went, the impending subversion would carry away the Republic."

It was a strange disturbance, beyond the experience of the government and the police. General Intelligence, the Nostradamus-Cassandra of the authorities, was somewhat at a loss, faced by an event generated not in the political and industrial spheres where its listening posts had long been well established but in the student body of the University of Paris, the Sorbonne. Its causes would be variously diagnosed and its course would not lend itself to clear-cut definition. It was blamed on international subversion, anarchical, involving the Communist extremes of Trotsky and Mao, for 1968 was a year of student protest across the world—in the United States, Japan, West Germany, Britain; some saw it as the revolt of youth against a middle-aged, ponderous regime, indifferent to their problems; others found in it the explosion of energies repressed by Gaullist authoritarianism. With hindsight, however, the outbreak seems to have been basically ad hoc, violence spontaneously multiplying and renewing itself, an astounding, bewildering outpouring of youthful eloquence creating an ephemeral, self-administering entity of revolt. Raymond Aron has called it *la révolution introuvable,* the undiscoverable revolution, an apt labeling of this amorphous and confusing rebellion. The men in ministerial office had no idea how to deal with it. It eluded their formulae, as it did those of the University of Paris.

The immediate origin of the May–June troubles was in student protest against the conditions of life under the antiquated tutelage of the Sorbonne, a clear case of old bottles and new wine. The university in recent years had admitted vast numbers of students for whom there were neither adequate academic facilities nor prospects of suitable employment after graduation. At the outset, Danny Cohn-Bendit, "Danny the Red," was to be the outstanding agitator and student leader but he was by no means the only young person who showed qualities of idealism and leadership during the weeks to come. The movement began in the Sorbonne's "overflow" campus in the stark suburb of Nanterre.

The Minister of the Interior, Christian Fouchet, a Gaullist stalwart since the London days, had already been worried by the weak handling of student protest by the academic administrations in Nantes and Strasbourg. The prime minister, Georges Pompidou, thought it was high time for a halt to be called to such incidents. General de Gaulle himself took a hand and told Fouchet that they must stop.

On May 3rd the university announced the closing of the Nanterre campus. The protesters thereupon came to Paris in force and made their gesture by occupying the sacrosanct courtyard of the Sorbonne. The rector of the university and the Minister of Education applied to the Prefect of Police for help. The Prefect, Maurice Grimaud, spoke on the telephone to the Minister of the Interior: "I do not like this business, but I have a requisition from the Rector, who is ill at ease, and Monsieur Peyrefitte's [Minister of Education's] cabinet are asking me to intervene. I don't see how I could refuse?"

"You could not refuse," said the minister, "besides, sooner or later, we shall have to come to it. Have the Sorbonne courtyard cleared, *Monsieur le Préfet,* without violence, of course, using the necessary resources."

The police cleared the courtyard without trouble, but then occurred one of those incidents that, misunderstood, provoke fierce reaction. As the students came out into the street the police shepherded them into buses so that they could be taken away to have their identity checked, a routine police procedure on such occasions. Other students, outside *en masse,* witnessing this, thought that their comrades had been arrested and at once, with incredible violence, started to attack the police. This was the first of a chain of events that would go on for six weeks. The Sorbonne was immediately reoccupied by students and not until those six weeks had gone by would the police pass through the great gateway again. On May 6th, four hundred demonstrators and two hundred police were injured in street fighting. Christian Fouchet wrote in his memoirs:

> In the memory of police officers—even among the old commissaires who remembered, when they were in the ranks, having gone through the 6th of February, 1934—such a tough confrontation had never been seen.... The riot lasted from 9.00 A.M. until late in the night. The police were able to maintain overall control. Twice, though, in telephone calls, I had sensed anxiety in Monsieur Grimaud's remarks, beneath his always even, calm voice. Twice, in fact, his forces had been in difficulties at certain points and he thought they were in danger of not being able to extricate themselves if they did not use their arms. The Prefect of Police believed, as I did, that at all costs a recourse to opening fire must be avoided. But it was not possible to let our forces get into an untenable position. I was obviously prepared to cover Monsieur Grimaud if he gave the order to fire. For I knew the Prefect of Police too well not to appreciate that he would not give that order unless he could not do otherwise. But I was also certain that the repercussions of that firing would make themselves heard all over the world.

The order to fire was never given.

Maurice Grimaud had been Director-General of the *Sûreté Nationale* for four years when he was appointed to be Prefect of Police in 1967. It was upon him that the onus of tackling the revolt primarily and most heavily fell. Fortunately, he had already agreed with the Secretary-General of the Police Nationale what their respective spheres of responsibility were, so the only higher authority to which he was subject was the Minister of the Interior and, above him, the prime minister and President de Gaulle. The prime minister, however, would be in Afghanistan until May 11th, whereupon the president went to Bucharest, not returning until May 18th.

Monsieur Grimaud had many advantages. He was a highly experienced member of the prefectoral corps, mature, intellectual and resilient. His composure, sincerity, and decisiveness inspired respect. He had a keen sense of history. His conception of his role in the maintenance of order was characterized by impartiality and reverence for law. He had the resources of the world's oldest urban police at his disposal. All these advantages would be turned to excellent account.

The objective was clear: the defense of Paris, the maintenance of order.

This meant firm opposition by his forces to young and lightly clad rioters, by no means uninstructed in the techniques of street fighting, able to scatter and concentrate again, to raise barricades and keep up a dangerous bombardment of missiles prized from the paving of streets and boulevards. In their protective gear the police had to move slowly—a hundred-yard charge was about the limit for riot-clad and equipped members of the Republican Security Companies. Their principal weapon was the tear-smoke grenade, thrown or fired, a nonlethal but effective agent of dispersal. The fury and strength of the rioters' onslaughts on occasion put a police station under siege but, though tactical police retreats had to be ordered, at no time were police formations overwhelmed. Television, curiously, made things worse for them, as youngsters watching the exciting action on the screen escaped from their homes to join in. This brought a new element of danger and difficulty: who would wish to find himself fighting *children* in a riot situation?

The Prefecture of Police's headquarters and local controls, which contrived by incessant updating of the operational map to keep track of many fluid situations, stood the test of unprecedented stress and strain. The Prefecture of Police's expertise was never seen to better advantage. The science of public-order maintenance has been intensively studied in France.

Certain principles, the wisdom of which is evident when May 1968 is contrasted with February 1934, were steadily adhered to in the deployment of the forces of order. One was that the police should never allow themselves to be cut off by being in too small groups. Another was that the operations would always be under the command of the civil police of Paris. Whether a formation consisted of a company of *gardiens de la paix* and a squadron of the Gendarmerie Mobile, or of Republican Security Companies with Gendarmerie Mobile squadrons, whatever the mixture, the command was always exercised by the Prefecture of Police's senior officers, whose knowledge of the city was a tremendous asset in the street operations.

As regards manpower, at first sight, the force available was impressive. The Prefect could draw on between six and eight thousand men for order maintenance from his own ranks. He could also draw on the Gendarmerie Mobile and the Republican Security Companies. In all, he had some twenty thousand men at his disposal. If a single major confrontation (like the confrontation in 1934) had been all that had to be dealt with, such force (if it could have been brought to bear in the labyrinthine city) would no doubt have been ample, but this was not one confrontation but many, taking place at any time of the day and sometimes of the night, and extending over a six-week period. Normally the pool on which the Prefect could draw over a twenty-four-hour span was ten thousand men. These could not all be used for street operations. There were vulnerable points to be guarded. And men often had to travel long distances from their homes, while the military police had to come from and return to outlying barracks. On a particular day, the Prefect would be able to put out 1,800 men in the morning, 1,600 in the afternoon, 1,350 in the evening. When reserves had to be drawn on to reinforce them, the fewer there would be for duty the following day. There was also the gravelling problem of the cumulatively increasing fatigue of men kept too long and too often on strenuous duty. The Prefect's watchword of the police's business being to maintain order, not to defeat an enemy, was not always observed by overtaxed and angry policemen.

There were instances, understandable but inexcusable, of excessive force used by police in the street and of violence towards persons detained on police premises, which went far towards alienating the public. Such instances the Prefect of Police had no intention of tolerating or disregarding. At the height of the struggle, to the dismay of certain high personages who were less concerned with ethics than expediency, who feared that the forces of order might be adversely affected at a critical moment, Maurice Grimaud sent a strong letter to every officer under his command. Plainspoken but heartfelt, it struck exactly the right note. An excerpt:

I know the trials that many of you have undergone. I know your bitterness over heartless remarks and persecutions of yourselves or your families, but the only way to change the deplorable attitude of some of the populace is to show yourselves in your true light and to wage pitiless war on those, fortunately not very numerous, who by their thoughtless actions would lend color to just that unfavorable image that people are trying to give us.

Far from alienating the men, the message was welcomed by the great majority and warmly endorsed by the police unions, with which the Prefect had been in frequent contact over working conditions during the emergency. The service was admirably officered, commissaires, *commandants,* and Gendarmerie officers always in firm front-line command, and those who led could always rely on a positive response to their demands. The Prefect was often to be found among units in action (as he was amid the demonstrators) where his understanding of the realities of the situation was hearteningly evident. Monsieur Grimaud had the gift, not as common as it might be among commanders, of being able to give praise where it was deserved. His memoirs most generously reflect his appreciation of those who shared the burden with him.

It is highly creditable that throughout the emergency, amid all its violence and destructiveness, communication with the demonstrators was always kept open. Commissaires would talk with student leaders in the street, telephone numbers in the police headquarters were given to the student "government," public-address equipment was loaned to marshals of student marches, accord was reached over the removal of casualties. Deals were made: on one occasion the students in charge at the Odéon Theater, which they had occupied, telephoned the Prefecture of Police to complain that the police had thrown tear-smoke grenades into the building. The Prefect's Chief of Cabinet pointed out that Molotov cocktails were being dropped on the police from housetops behind the theater: he said that if this stopped, so would the grenades. Agreement! The oft-repeated assurance that the police were not there to suppress the student movement but to maintain order for the people of Paris also had a gradual effect on the temper of the rising.

The student riots were complicated for the police by industrial action taken by the trade unions. Though the two movements were of totally different kinds, with little significant coalescence taking place, the incidence of organized labor's demonstrations, marches, and strikes made heavy additional demands on the order-maintenance forces. The emergency was all the more grave by reason of this massive further opposition to the government.

On May 29th, General de Gaulle vanished. Even the prime minister was in the dark as to his whereabouts and intentions. The dissolution of the Chamber of Deputies was thought to be imminent. Meanwhile, the CGT, the General Workers' Union, in Communist obedience, mustered 100,000 people to march in Paris. Happily, the demonstration was well-organized and peaceful.

Late that afternoon the general, who had been away to assure himself of the army's support, was reported back at his country home, Colombey-les-Deux-Eglises. Noon of the next day found him in Paris at the Elysée Palace. It was announced that he would broadcast at 4.30 P.M. A counterdemonstration by the Gaullists had been called for 6.00 P.M. on the Place de la Concorde, but as the general had spoken once before during the emergency, and then to little effect, it was thought that the broadcast would not influence the demonstration.

But that afternoon, when he spoke, the general was on his greatest and grandest form. The Concorde demonstration, which had been expected to attract about 25,000 people, now became the rallying point for "the silent majority." Several hundred thousand people assembled. Their meeting gave the government a clear mandate to resolve the emergency.

The emergency, nevertheless, was by no means over. Rioting in Paris, sporadic but dangerous, continued. It took a commissaire of police, three Republican Security Companies, and a bulldozer until 4.00 A.M. on June 11th to clear the boulevard Saint-Michel. That was the fiercest encounter since May 24th, but it was to be the last.

The Odéon was peacefully cleared by the police. General de Gaulle asked the Prefect of Police to clear the Sorbonne. It was no light matter to disagree with the president but the Prefect thought such a move would be premature. He therefore waited until June 16th, when he went himself to talk with the student committee. At 5.30 P.M. the students made a ceremonial and orderly exist.

President de Gaulle undoubtedly dealt the crushing blow to

the revolt by his broadcast on May 30th. But from May 3rd, until that crucial moment of reaction, it had been the forces of order under Maurice Grimaud who had defended the Republic. But for his policies, and the manner in which they were carried out, it is not too much to say that the Fifth Republic would have perished in the spring of 1968.

How many police forces in the world could have stood up to such sustained disorder? If it sometimes appears to the foreign observer that France has an inordinate amount of police strength in order-maintenance reserve, perhaps Paris's experience in those days might be remembered.

Another Era

The succession of governments from 1958 to 1981 constitute the Gaullist era, though Charles de Gaulle died in 1970. In the summer of 1981 another era, still within the framework of the Constitution of 1958, began with the election of a Socialist, François Mitterand, as president of France.

To date, this has brought no radical revision of the police system. The major change in the administrative sphere has been to give a new title and a modified role to the high officials who have been known as Prefects since the time of Napoleon. These are now designated Commissaires of the Republic. Their previous power over local government has been reduced to give greater scope to the elected local authorities. The Commissaire of the Republic nevertheless has the same police powers and responsibilities as the Prefects before him. In Paris there is still a Prefect of Police, and in Lyon, Marseille, and Lille there are still Prefects delegated to be in charge of the police.

Considerable change, however, had taken place in police affairs during the last twelve years of the Gaullist era. Women, hitherto admitted only to "assistant" status, at last began to be accepted for regular appointments in the Police Nationale and the Gendarmerie.

"Gendarmettes," as they were inevitably nicknamed, have been recruited on a voluntary basis since 1974. They serve as secretaries, switchboard operators, interpreters, or first-aiders.

THE GENDARMERIE NATIONALE

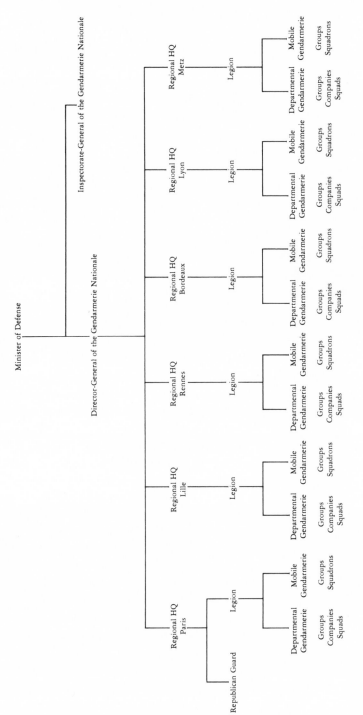

111

3

About five hundred have been admitted. They are eligible for promotion to noncommissioned rank.

The Police Nationale took a more liberal view of what functions might be allotted to women, though they have expressed reservations, holding that many police duties are physically unsuited to them. Since 1974 women have been eligible for appointment as commissaires of police, since 1970 as *inspecteurs* (plain-clothes officers) and since 1973 as *enquêteurs* (investigators). In 1975 some 4,500 women were working in the police service, but most of these were in the "assistant" category, without police powers. In that year, 4 women were accepted for training as commissaires of police, 254 as *inspecteurs,* and 136 as *enquêteurs.* Not until 1978 were women allowed to join the uniform branch as *gardiens de la paix,* when fifty-one out of a thousand candidates were accepted.

The corps of *enquêteurs* came into legal existence in 1972, the title giving a slightly inflated idea of what their duties entail. They work under the authority of the commissaires of police, keeping observation, making inquiries, and serving auxiliary purposes in air and frontier police work. They have certain powers in connection with road traffic accidents. They do not wear uniform or carry arms.

In 1969, to cope with the great increase in business at airports and frontier crossings, the Air and Frontier Police became a separate uniformed corps within the Police Nationale. They were then placed under the General Intelligence directorate but in 1972 were removed to the immediate supervision of the Director-General. Among their responsibilities is cooperation with the Directorate of Urban Police (for questions of public order), the Directorate of Criminal Investigation (dangerous drugs and international criminals), and the DST for surveillance of persons whose activities might affect national security. They have antiterrorist units at the airports.

CHAPTER 8

Organization

THE GROWTH OF France's police systems has been outlined in the last six chapters, in the context of French history. At this point it will be timely to give some account of the lines on which the police systems of today are organized.

Flic Numéro Un

The idea of having a Minister of Police has found little favor in France since the days of Napoleon and, like most countries, on both sides of the Iron Curtain and in the Third World, the French prefer to place their police under other ministers. Perhaps there is something repugnant in the notion of a political minister solely occupied with police, with its implication of an undesirable concentration of force in the hands of a single person, though New Zealand, a country of exemplary civic freedom, is apparently able to reconcile itself to having a Minister of Police. So, incidentally, is South Africa. The French, like the Italians, have found it fitting to distribute the control of the police among no less than three ministers.

The Minister of the Interior has administrative control of the civil police. The Minister of Defense has similar control of the Gendarmerie. The Minister of Justice, in the relationships of both civil and military police to the criminal justice system, represents the judicial control of the police in the investigation and the proof of crime.

Of these three, the most important is the Minister of the Interior, whose precedence of the Minister of Defense lies not so much in controlling a more numerous police as in the civil power being able to requisition military force, so that, in a very real sense, the Gendarmerie are always at the disposal of the civil authorities. Those authorities are mainly supervised by the Minister of the Interior, whose business is by no means limited to the police, being concerned also with central government's dealings with local administration, mainly involving the commissaires of the Republic, the elected councils, and the mayors. The more spectacular of his roles, however, is as head of the police, *"flic numéro un,"* "top cop," as Georges Clemenceau put it.

The personality and policies of an individual Minister of the Interior can have very considerable effects on the police. His influence in the inner councils of the government counts for a good deal, particularly in budgetary matters. To take a fairly recent example, Raymond Marcellin, in office from 1968 to 1974, coming in at the tail end of the 1968 riots, was able to embark upon a vigorous policy of increased recruitment, creating over 18,000 jobs in five years. His belief in carrying a big stick and waving it about, however, diverted much of the new strength into the reserves held ready for public disorder.

A former subordinate of the harsh postwar Minister of the Interior Jules Moch, Marcellin was intensely conscious of the possibilities of further tumult after the suppression of the May riots. With Jules Moch in 1948 he had seen the overwhelming deployment of Republican Security Companies, regular civil police and the Gendarmerie, with other military support, 45,000 men, to concentrate at the scene of coal strikes in Northern France. In two weeks the emergency ended, from which he seems to have concluded that force is the answer. Once in power, he set about proving it.

Factories and other industrial establishments in lock-out or strike situations, demonstrations, marches, wherever the shadow of public disorder loomed, Marcellin sent in his forces. He ordered the expulsion of aliens, dissolved what he thought were subversive groups, banned meetings and assemblies, taking full advantage of the reactionary climate prevailing after the May riots. His inveterate suspicion of "red" plots provoked intensive police action, involving interminable meetings in the ministry of senior officers of the police, military, and intelligence services. He sought to have arrested the leaders of student revolutionary groups that he had dissolved and was dissuaded only when told that there was no legal justification for such measures. He formed regional investigative squads staffed with General Intelligence officers, a serious departure from the branch's informative function, using them for repressive police action. (His successor, Michel Poniatowski, lost no time in putting a stop to this.) His policy, it had to be admitted, enabled some long-sought political malefactors to be brought to justice.

It was during Marcellin's period of office as Minister of the Interior that the reduction of the Prefecture of Police to parity with the former *Sûreté Nationale* was finally engineered. If the *Sûreté* lost its title, the Prefecture of Police, as already mentioned, lost in more substantial ways.

The new broom of the Marcellin administration certainly swept a good deal towards the Police Nationale in the way of manpower, reorganization, and resources and his tenure of office demonstrates the power of a political minister to influence, orient, and reshape the police machine.

In 1982, by presidential decree of September 1st, the Minister of the Interior and of Decentralization (as the office has been called since the accession of François Mitterand to power) has delegated his control of the Police Nationale to a Secretary of State in Charge of Public Security. The new minister will now sign on behalf of the Minister of the Interior and of Decentralization all decrees and other instruments concerning the police.

The Police Nationale

Under the political control of the Minister of the Interior and of Decentralization, and the Secretary of State in Charge of Public

Security, the chief police executive is the Director-General of the Police Nationale, a prefect, member of one of France's elite administrative corps. From his headquarters in the rue des Saussaies in central Paris, he and the senior officials of his staff administer the civil police service of France. His immediate staff (cabinet) includes a colonel of the Gendarmerie Nationale as liaison officer.

Some account of the Director-General's headquarters and its relationship to the functioning of the police follows.*

ATTACHED SERVICES

Three services are directly attached to the Director-General's own office. These are the Central Automobile Service (police transportation resources), the Security Service of the Ministry of the Interior (protection of ministerial premises), and the Central Sports Service of the Police Nationale.

CENTRAL "EXTERNAL" SERVICES

Two "external" services are also central. The Inspectorate-General of the Police Nationale is staffed by a Director, Inspectors-General, and Controllers-General, assisted by commissaires of police. At various times this service has been attached to the cabinet of the Minister of the Interior but it is now immediately under the Director-General of the Police Nationale.

The Inspectorate-General's business is "internal affairs," "the policing of the police." In days gone by it was felt that to bring a police officer, however peccant, before the courts would harm the police's standing in the eyes of the public to an extent far in excess of any benefit to be obtained by his conviction. That has not been so in recent years. The past decade has seen a new rigor both in the criminal prosecution of police officers and in the service's own disciplinary sanctions. The Inspectorate-General is concerned not only with integrity but also with efficiency. Guy Denis, who was its

*Jean-Pierre Arrighi and Bernard Grasso give a meticulous analysis of police organization in their *La Police Nationale, Missions et Structures* (1979).

Director at the time of his writing *Citoyen Policier,* records that in 1974, 2,404 punishments were inflicted within the service: 1,063 cautions, 913 reprimands, 203 dismissals, 108 transfers, 65 definitive and 38 temporary suspensions, and 22 demotions.

The Official Travel and Security of High Personages Service makes the security arrangements for the journeys of the president of the Republic and for those of other high personages, both French and foreign. It is staffed by a director, a controller-general, and commissaires of police of varying grades.

Administrative Directorates

There are three administrative directorates in the Police Nationale's headquarters. The title of the Directorate of Personnel and Matériel is sufficiently explanatory of its functions. The Directorate of Regulations and Legal Affairs is concerned with the Minister of the Interior's regulation making in respect of such matters as aliens and traffic, and with claims and disputes. The Directorate of Training deals with the police's extensive and complex training system, which is discussed in Chapter 9 below.

Operational Directorates

Seven directorates in the headquarters control and coordinate the operational work of the police.

1. The Central Directorate of General Intelligence performs this function for the branch of the police that has the mission of seeking and communicating political, social, and economic intelligence for the information of the government. The service is deployed on a regional basis, with units at departmental level feeding the regional headquarters with information so that a daily synthesis may be submitted to the Central Directorate in Paris. Here there are three subdirectorates.

The Sub-Directorate of General Political Information studies the activities of political parties and monitors the mass media. It is, in the words of Jules Moch, "the meteorologist of public opinion." The Sub-Directorate of Social Information studies unions, socioeconomic conditions and trends, student activities, the financial world, oversea colonies and international affairs. The Sub-Directorate of Racecourses and Gambling may seem something of a misfit, for the work here is more of a regular police order than of the order of an intelligence service, but its members are ranked as General Intelligence personnel. If asked what conceivable interest a person's playing roulette could possibly have for the government, they would possibly reply that the person in question might be a factory owner staking tomorrow's payroll: political, social, and economic consequences could stem from a run of bad luck!

The information amassed at the department level is placed at the disposal of the departmental Commissaire of the Republic (in Paris, of the Prefect of Police), the Prefect of the Defense Zone, the Director of General Intelligence, and the Minister of the Interior.

The nature of the information collected, either directly by the officers of the service or through its innumerable contacts, is varied in the extreme. The dates, times, and places of meetings are charted ahead, with their objects, speakers, and estimated attendance. When the meeting takes place a report is made on the proceedings. In certain cases, General Intelligence will give warning to the authorities responsible for the maintenance of order so that the necessary measures may be taken. Election campaigns are intensely studied and General Intelligence parliamentary election forecasts have proved remarkably accurate. General Intelligence gave precise warning of the insurrection in Algiers on November 1, 1954, the date on which the long emergency began, and, through a telephone intercept, of the rising there in April 1961. Background checks on individuals, such as those seeking to enter public service, are exhaustively conducted, a task facilitated by France's long tradition of documenting her citizens. A dossier is kept on each department, in which the categories of information required by the Central Directorate are kept up to date, reflecting, inter alia, the political scene in the municipalities, with particulars of the aliens in the area and the biographies of persons who have come to notice. Where instances arise in which, say, crime or espionage may be involved, the appropriate Criminal Investigation or Counter-Espionage service is informed. Regular liaison is maintained with other branches of the Police Nationale and with the Gendarmerie.

Sophisticated communications and data processing are obviously essential to the success of operations of such delicacy and volume. These resources French governments with an insatiable appetite for knowing what is going on have provided.

2. The central directorate that in England or America would be called the detective or criminal investigation department has a title which, literally translated, is "The Central Directorate of Judicial Police." Though it has been referred to here as "Criminal Investigation" when previously mentioned, and will be so referred to throughout, it is apposite to note that the expression *police judiciaire* designates sometimes a function and sometimes the service that performs the function and in current usage means the function of establishing that breaches of the criminal law have been committed, seeking the perpetrators and the proofs, and bringing them to the notice of the judicial authorities.

The Central Directorate of Criminal Investigation controls and coordinates the Police Nationale's detective work. The Director ranks as France's chief detective and is head of France's National Central Bureau of Interpol, the International Criminal Police Organization, described in Chapter 10 below.

The headquarters is largely but not entirely administrative in character, dealing with such personnel matters as assignments, in-branch finance (the close scrutiny of detectives' expense accounts is never neglected in any police headquarters anywhere, regardless of the state of crime), and allotment of vehicles and equipment. Coordination of detective activities, however, implies much more than mere administration: the Director and his aides can and do participate in operations.

Some services are immediately under the Director. One of these is for liaison with the Gendarmerie, a function performed by a joint staff of civil and military police officers, very necessary where there are so many possibilities of trespassing upon one another's preserves and of wasteful duplication of inquiries. Another is the Central Service of Judicial Identification, which deals not only with the establishment of identity by fingerprinting, photography, and what remains of Bertillon's anthropometric techniques, but also with the work of the police laboratories, including document examination, ballistics, scene-of-crime traces, and photo- and identi-kits.

The Sub-Directorate of General Services and Liaison provides a legal research and criminal statistics service; it has computerized means of handling information about crime and criminals, with such built-in factors as *modus operandi* (i.e., the mode in which a crime is committed, which can often narrow a search to particular suspects). The Sub-Directorate circulates information on persons brought to notice by law-enforcement agencies nationwide.

The Sub-Directorate of Criminal Affairs deals with banditry and procuring for prostitution, offenses against persons and property, offenses against the security of the state, subversion, and narcotics. "Banditry" in this context includes gang crime, aggravated theft, protection rackets, and kidnapping. The Sub-Directorate is called upon for expert assistance in certain cases, thus participating in operational inquiries; it is organized to provide this service both locally and at an international level.

The Sub-Directorate of Economic and Financial Affairs deals with "white-collar" crime, false pretenses, counterfeiting, and forgery, including art forgery.

Each of the subdirectorates is regarded as having a preventive as well as a repressive role. Crime prevention in France has developed a new impetus since the time when Michel Poniatowski took the portfolio of the Ministry of the Interior.

The work of the Regional Crime Services—the Regional Crime Squads initiated by Hennion and Sébille having been thus renamed in 1947—is controlled from the Central Directorate of Criminal Investigation. There are now nineteen such services, referred to in France as the "SRPJ"—*services régionaux de police judiciaire.* The Paris service is described in some detail in Chapter 7 above. The role of the Regional Crime Services is to make inquiries into organized, professional, and itinerant crime, in liaison with the kindred services of the Central Directorate, and to coordinate the investigations made at local level by the urban police, over whom they have authority in matters concerning the more serious criminal offenses. Each of the nineteen services has jurisdiction within a region, their territory being that of an Appeal Court, to whose Prosecutor-General they are specifically linked. A region contains several territorial departments: the Regional Crime Service with headquarters in Toulouse, for instance, covers seven departments, the one in Lyon, eight, and the one in Lille, five.

Their Paris headquarters contains specialist sections concentrating on aspects of major crime and enjoys the investigative and other resources mentioned above in connection with the Central Directorate. The most important service rendered by their headquarters in the capital is probably through its central criminal records system, which makes information available on a regional basis to the local investigators. As with all such systems, it operates on a two-way basis, the information it is able to diffuse depending largely on the quality and quantity of the information that its clientele, the regional services, are able to feed into it.

3. The Central Directorate of Urban Police is concerned with the police stationed in cities and circumscriptions. Their business is the maintenance of order, public safety, tranquillity, and salubrity. They protect persons and property. In a small city there will usually only be a single commissaire of police, with uniformed and plain-clothes personnel under his authority. He acts in both the administrative and the criminal police spheres. In a large city, all the major operational directorates—Urban Police, Criminal Investigation, General Intelligence, Counter-Espionage—will generally be represented. The chief of the urban police there is called the Central Commissaire, and he has under his command commissaires of police of *quartiers* with their small units of uniformed and plain-clothes officers, a main body of urban police in uniform, and the city detective department. The last-named, commanded by a commissaire whose grade is in proportion to the size of the department, is charged with judicial and administrative affairs, crime prevention, social protection (morals, narcotics, minors, aliens), and criminal records. All the personnel, who are *inspecteurs,* are in plain clothes. In criminal matters, the city detective department takes cognizance of all that occurs within the city limits. It informs the regional crime service of all important cases. Where a case extends beyond those limits the regional crime service takes over, with the assistance of a city detective. This procedure avoids overlapping, and good coordination brings good results. Here one sees the value of a national police system: the urban police inform

121

the regional crime service, which in turn transmits any important intelligence to the Central Directorate in Paris. The latter, in certain cases, circulates it throughout the country, and this can lead to cross-checks and association of data. Thus, the usefulness of centralization, coordination, and cooperation becomes clear. Another feature of a national police may be emphasized: specialization. Each branch has a defined mission—political, economic, social intelligence, burglary, fraud, counterfeiting, dangerous drugs, counterespionage, and so on, and makes available its expertise to the police services nationwide.

The urban police, except in Paris, Lyon and the Rhône, Marseille and the Bouches du Rhône, and Lille and the Nord, where the Prefect of Police and the Prefects Delegated for Police respectively have control, are under the authority of the departmental Commissaire of the Republic, though the day-to-day oversight is a matter for the departmental Director of Urban Police. The Central Directorate in Paris is responsible for organization, operation, and personnel assignments.

4. The Central Service of the Republican Security Companies constitutes a separate branch of the Police Nationale, whose chief is directly responsible to the Director-General for the Companies' organization, training, and operation.

The sixty-one companies of the CRS are a formidable riot reserve. Their authorized strength is 87 commissaires of police, 434 *commandants* and *officiers de paix* of all grades, and 15,157 *gardiens de la paix* and noncommissioned officers. The sixty-one companies are formed into ten groups, the group commanders being responsible to the Chief of the Central Service in the Director-General's headquarters. Their riot function is always foremost in the mind of the public, though the personnel of the companies are frequently employed as lifeguards, in mountain rescue, and in work with juveniles, in addition to their main extra functions in the policing of airports and in urban traffic control.

In his novel *En Face les C.R.S* (C.R.S. to the Front), Robert Mungoli, writing from his own experience as a CRS officer, has one of his characters, a company commander, say to his junior officers:

> The maintenance of order isn't war, the demonstrators aren't enemies, at most adversaries. And if war has no laws.... the mainte-

122

nance of order has, and they are strict. Our actions depend most of the time on a decision which isn't ours, a decision of people who don't know us and who handle us like dynamite, fear us a little or a lot: they have hidden us in the cellars or brandished us as a terrible threat: "If you don't behave, I'll fetch the C.R.S." as one might say, "I'm turning my dogs loose." But never forget, in spite of everything, that there are rules, and they must be respected, inept as they may seem to you.

The activation of the CRS in normal circumstances (i.e., when twenty-four hours' notice of the need for them can be given) is authorized, or refused, when the Commissaire of the Republic requests their aid. In an emergency, a Commissaire of the Republic may activate any CRS in his department. In the case of an unexpected major incident, the local police chief can demand CRS assistance. In such cases the Commissaire of the Republic will inform both the minister and the Prefect of the Defense Zone.

5. The function of the Directorate of Counter-Espionage is to ensure that the activities of foreign inspiration of a kind to harm the interests of France are repressed. The Directorate controls an intelligence service in the field of counterespionage within France's frontiers, a security service that aims to protect the national secrets, and a "field" service that investigates and performs the police part of the process leading to prosecution in cases of espionage.

In countering spying today the problem is not so much to prevent the plans of the fort being stolen as it is to safeguard the innumerable secrets of France's scientific, technical, and economic resources. The policing of radio-electric communications falls to the Counter-Espionage Service, where the process of detecting breaches of the law governing such communications is propitious for intercepting clandestine transmissions by foreign agents.

The Counter-Espionage Service is covered by official secrecy and no details of its organizational structure or personnel are given.

6. The Central Service of the Air and Frontier Police controls the movement of people and foreign publications to and from French territory, protects persons and property, and collects information incidental to these activities. The Air and Frontier Police,

under their Chief, come directly under the control of the Director-General of the Police Nationale.

Their business, working both in uniform and plain clothes, is to enforce the law in general and the laws regarding their own missions in particular, as well as to act protectively. They investigate air and rail accidents, undertake police inquiries of all kinds, and enter into the policing of aliens. The more serious cases are passed to the appropriate services of the Central Directorate of Criminal Investigation. Their work naturally involves questions of security as well as of crime, public order as well as aircraft regulations, and liaison is maintained accordingly with other branches. The CRS assist in the uniform policing of airports.

7. The Service of International Technical Co-operation deals with the training in France of police officers from other countries. It also provides advisory services to foreign police forces. France has been active in promoting such technical relationships, especially with her former possessions.

MONOLITH

The outline that has just been traced reflects the extent to which the French civil police system has developed into a monolithic organization.

In any such structure, the balance of initiative is precariously held between the highly bureaucratized superstructure and the operational organisms "on the ground." Advocates of nationalized police systems will point to economies of size, to the central provision and distribution of resources, the value of standardization, coordination and specialization. The police pragmatist, nevertheless may doubt whether it is right to have so much remote control of what is fundamentally a localized business, dependent for its immediate efficacy on local knowledge and local initiative. When what could be settled round the parish pump has to be interminably referred to far-away officials (in more than a geographical sense), the pragmatist can only sigh. The vaunted economies of size often in practice have the effect of taking more people out of the line for staff duties and increase the appalling volume of paperwork on which centralized administration help-lessly depends.

In the United States, such centralized control, besides being anathema to the citizenry, is, as the Constitution stands, legally impossible. Even if the Constitution were amended to permit it, state and local authorities would fight tooth and nail to hang on to their traditional police power. In Britain, the temptation to nationalize the police may prove very much more difficult to resist.

The Gendarmerie Nationale

The fine military style of the Gendarmerie Nationale must not be allowed to obscure the fact that the Gendarmerie is a sophisticated and highly successful police force.* Its systems of recruitment and training guarantee a high standard of personnel in all ranks and its buildings and equipment are of a quality that most police forces must envy. Light aircraft and helicopters are in regular use from their regional headquarters. Criminal records are computerized. A central photographic system provides twenty-four-hour service throughout the country. The policing of France's immense flow of road traffic is facilitated by a national center, informing also the Police Nationale, which rapidly circulates traffic data down to the needed levels.

The main functions of the force are the policing of the smaller communities and the preservation of the public peace when it is in danger. The overall organization that ensures they are performed reflects true military order and method. It should not be forgotten that management was a military art long before it stumbled into industry and commerce.

At national level, responsible to the Minister of Defense, the Gendarmerie is controlled by a Director-General. At first sight, it may seem odd that this office is not held by a high military officer but by a high civil official, just as the Police Nationale's Director-General's post is held not by a career police officer but by a

---

*For an admirably detailed and up-to-date book on the military police of France, see J.R.J. Jammes, *Effective Policing: The French Gendarmerie* (1982).

member of the prefectoral corps. The present Director-General is a member of that corps. His predecessor was a judge and before him was a high official of the Ministry of Justice.

At national level, too, is the Inspectorate-General, this time under military command, rating a general, who reports directly to the Minister of Defense on the state of the force.

The Director-General does not only control the Gendarmerie's police system; he is also in charge of Gendarmerie on duties overseas and in West Germany and Berlin, and of provost police with the armed forces in France. Directly attached to his office are the central administrative and technical services.

At the highest operational level, the Gendarmerie has a Regional Headquarters in each of France's six Defense Zones. All the gendarmes in the region constitute a Legion, which thus comprises Departmental Gendarmerie and Gendarmerie Mobile. While the latter are liable to be moved to anywhere in France, the Departmental Gendarmerie are permanently stationed in a particular region. The Republican Guard is permanently stationed in Paris.

The Regional Headquarters of the Mobile Gendarmerie has several squadrons under its command, each of 135 men. The Regional Headquarters of the Departmental Gendarmerie has under it groups of companies, under which individual companies come under command, and each company is divided into *brigades* (squads). The network of squads is vast; there are 3,678 of them stationed all over France. Their size varies according to the population of their jurisdiction.

A region contains several territorial departments, themselves subdivided into *arrondissements* (districts). An *arrondissement* contains communes (municipalities with elected councils and mayors) and cantons (electoral districts). The headquarters of the companies of the Departmental Gendarmerie are usually situated in the largest commune of an *arrondissement*. At company level there are a criminal investigation unit and a reserve platoon for emergency and other duties. All gendarmes are required to live in military quarters. This may sound restrictive, but they are often better housed than their civil-police counterparts. The *brigades* are stationed in the main town of the canton.

The Gendarmerie is in contact with the civil authorities at several levels. On the administrative side, the Director-General is in direct touch with the Minister of Defense; the general commanding in the region with the Prefect of the Defense Zone; the colonel commanding in the Department with the Commissaire of the Republic; the company commander with the Deputy Commissaire of the Republic in the *arrondissement;* and the commander of the *brigade* with the mayor of the commune. On the judicial side, in criminal investigation, the Gendarmerie officers come under the control of the Public Prosecutors and the *juges d'instruction* in the same way as Police Nationale officers on detective duty.

If a comparison is to be made of France's two great police systems, the most striking difference is probably in their relative visibility. The *presence* of the police is far more evident in the case of the Gendarmerie. The very nature of their deployment explains this. Spread as they are over 95 percent of France's surface, the great majority of them serving in the Departmental Gendarmerie, living with their families in the midst of the populace, always wearing uniform, continually on patrol, regularly seen (if not always welcomed) by the motorist, the gendarmes are inevitably the best-known police in France. The Gendarmerie is not as numerous as the Police Nationale, the present strength being about 84,000, of which 17,000 are in the Mobile Gendarmerie, 3,000 in the Republican Guard and 2,000 on provost and specialist duties.

In the long view, harmonious cooperation between the Police Nationale and the Gendarmerie can only be to the advantage of both and of the public they serve. People intent upon their individual, detailed work, however, do not always take the long view and are much more inclined to take the short one. Police officers in all ages have been constitutionally reluctant to share their hard-won knowledge. Vidocq wrote that a policeman should tell his ideas to nobody, "not even to the Almighty." It is hardly to be avoided that when two distinct organizations, heirs of very different traditions, are pursuing the same ends, there will be competition and rivalry. Whatever may appear on paper in the form of instructions regarding liasion, and whatever may be said by lofty hierarchs, the old Adam will emerge sooner or later. When conditions of service in the two organizations are also markedly different, antipathies are bound to exist.

Edmond Sébeille, writing of the period when he was a commissaire in the Regional Crime Service of Marseille, recounts in his *L'Affaire Dominici* that, when he was investigating the murders of Sir Jack and Lady Drummond and their little daughter, his chief came out to visit him at the scene of the crime. As it had taken place in the countryside, the case had at first been in the hands of the Gendarmerie. Their captain remarked to the detective chief that it would not be an easy one to clear up. The man from Marseille responded, somewhat unfortunately, "Obviously, otherwise you wouldn't have sent for us." This did nothing to improve Sébeille's relations with the gendarmes, who did not thereafter put themselves out to be helpful. Sébeille also found that the *juge d'instruction* in the initial stages of the inquiry had issued rogatory commissions to the Gendarmerie, resulting in reports and statements that he had not seen.

Among the sources of friction between the Police Nationale and the Gendarmerie have been the growth of towns and the outgrowth of suburbs. A town of nine thousand population expands to over ten thousand; in theory the policing should pass to the Police Nationale. But the Gendarmerie, having policed the area since time immemorial, see no reason why they should now withdraw, and given administrative inertia in high places (usually a safe bet), they will probably keep their turf. A similar situation arises as suburbs develop, the city expanding into the countryside, into territory long policed by the Gendarmerie, while the Police Nationale regard the suburbs as part of *their* jurisdiction. Friction may also be caused when members of either force pursue fleeing suspects into each other's preserves.

These are not very grave incompatibilities. Both systems have learned to live with them.

CHAPTER 9

The Police Career

The Police Nationale

RECRUITMENT

Entry to the regular police forces of Britain and the United States is always in the former, and almost always in the latter, by way of appointment as a uniformed officer. The French would not think it sensible to follow this practice. It would be unrealistic in France to expect people with high academic qualifications to join the police at the same level and for the same remuneration as people who have barely scraped through high school. Nor would it be accepted that people who are otherwise well qualified for investigative or other specialist duties should be excluded because they do not meet a minimum height requirement appropriate for the needs of the uniformed service. It is clear to the French that police work is of great variety, that some people are better suited to one kind of work than to another, and that it is therefore most economical and productive to direct them from the outset onto what seems the best path for their particular abilities rather than to start them all off on the same footing.

It is often argued in America and in Britain that the soundest way to begin a police career is in uniform, in the presence of the public, that it is in daily contact with people and their troubles and the troubles that people cause that the police apprenticeship is most usefully served. It is argued, too, that this initial quality of entrants to the service promotes solidarity and good understanding among the different levels of the hierarchy, and gives the higher ranks an insight into the work and feelings of their subordinates that they could have gained in no other way. Every commander of a police force in the United Kingdom (and Ireland) today, and there are fifty-one forces, joined the service in the lowest rank.

The argument that the armed forces of the United States and Britain recruit their commissioned officers as cadets and give them high-quality training at world-famous officer-cadet academies such as West Point and Sandhurst and do not make them spend years in the lower ranks is countered by pointing out that police are not soldiers and that the officer on patrol has powers over his or her fellow citizens that even a five-star general does not possess. A police officer's decision made in a street emergency may occupy the higher judiciary for years in trying to establish whether what the officer did was legal. It is a cogent reply, in the context of the different objectives of the two kinds of service. And it is only fair to say that not all members of the French police, senior or junior, believe that their system of direct recruitment to higher ranks is on the right lines. To consider the question it is first necessary to see just what those lines are.

Certain general requirements must be satisfied by candidates for the French police service. As with all civil-service appointments in France, entry is in every case by competitive examination. Those seeking to join must be of French nationality or have been naturalized for five years. They must have fulfilled their obligations to national service. Their eyesight must be good but for service in the uniform branch must not need correction by glasses. They must be free from any physical condition that might be incompatible with the performance of police duty and be of a constitution sufficiently robust to stand up to its hardships (this is relaxed where office duties are concerned). An official medical examination is mandatory. The possession of full civil rights and good character is essential, and they must be accepted by the responsible Prefect in the Director-General's administration. No one may take the competitive examination more than three times. A thorough background check is made.

Recruitment is to one of the five corps of police personnel. In ascending order, these are:

First, as an *enquêteur* (investigator). The age limits are nineteen to twenty-eight years, the latter extended for those who have performed national service. It will be remembered that France still has conscription, the draft. No academic certificates are required but candidates must take a competitive examination at high-school level.

Second, as a *gardien de la paix,* the equivalent of a constable or police officer in uniform. The age limits again are nineteen to twenty-eight years, with extension for national service. This time there is a minimum height requirement, 1 meter, 68 centimeters. No academic certification is required but candidates must take a competitive examination at higher primary education level.

Third, as an *officier de paix,* the basic supervisory rank of the uniform branch, similar to a police lieutenant in New York City or an inspector in London. There are two ways to reach this rank: one directly from outside the service, the other by qualifying for promotion from the uniform ranks. The exterior candidates must be from nineteen to twenty-eight years of age, with extension for national service. The minimum height requirement is 1 meter, 68 centimeters. They must have an academic certificate more or less equivalent to the American "associate" degree or the British "A" levels. They have to take a competitive examination in such subjects as general culture and public law. The in-service candidates compete for 50 percent of the vacant posts. Of these, 25 percent are reserved for men holding noncommissioned rank, aged at least forty-five; the other 25 percent are reserved for men who have at least four years' service in the Police Nationale, aged not more than thirty-five years, with extension for national service. Physical aptitude is strictly required in the case of anyone not serving in the corps of *gardiens de la paix.*

Fourth, as an *inspecteur,* a plain-clothes officer. Again, there are two ways to reach the rank. Exterior candidates must be aged twenty-one to thirty years, with extension for national service. The educational requirements may be roughly equated with the American "associate" degree or English "A" levels. The interior candidates must have four years' service in the Police Nationale and be no more than thirty-five years of age. The competitive examination is in such subjects as general culture, public and penal law, and history. Vacancies are allotted 50 percent to exterior and 50 percent to in-service candidates.

Fifth, as a *commissaire of police,* the basic command rank. There are two ways to reach this. Exterior candidates must be aged twenty-one to thirty years, with extension for national service. They must have university higher degrees or the equivalent. In-service candidates must be serving police officers or administrative secretaries eligible for police service, with at least four years' service and under thirty-five years of age, with extension for national service. The competitive examination is at a high level, with questions on general culture, administrative law, penal law, and penal procedure. The vacancies competed for are reserved 45 percent for exterior and 55 percent for in-service candidates. The latter quota is apportioned 20 percent for in-service candidates as mentioned above, and 35 percent for officers whom it is desired to reward for their services; these are often approaching their fiftieth year, but must take the same training program as the others at the *Ecole Nationale Supérieure de Police.*

The French recruitment system thus has the advantage of recruiting well-qualified young people to its higher ranks without depriving those already serving of the opportunity to advance to senior posts.

TRAINING

Police training in France has been going on longer than in the United States or Britain. The Prefecture of Police had a school for newly joined probationers as long ago as 1883, the *Ecole Pratique* (School of Practice) *des gardiens de la paix,* which had a continuous life until the consolidation of the training systems of the Prefecture of Police and the *Sûreté Nationale* which began in 1968. The

Ecole Technique (School of Technique) *de Police* of the Prefecture of Police began in 1895 in Bertillon's department; it was reconstituted in 1935 and branched out into the training of *inspecteurs* and of student-commissaires of police, also into specialist training. The *Sûreté Nationale* had no professional training until the founding of the *Ecole Nationale Supérieure de Police* in 1941. The higher training of the Police Nationale is now concentrated there.

With the whole police training system now under the control of the Director-General of the Police Nationale, it has been possible to design a coherent structure with common principles governing what is done in the many component establishments. The art and science of police cannot be learned in academia, though academia may contribute to their study in valuable ways; in-service inculcation of the techniques, practice, and ethos of police is irreplaceable. It is also necessary, in-service, to teach and reemphasize that police work has to be done amid a changing society, wherein police operate in the service of their fellow citizens. The latter considerations demand, as the French have realized, a fair amount of social and civic study in all basic training programs. As all uniformed police carry firearms and all in plain clothes are entitled to do so, the *enquêteurs* excepted, weapon training (instruction and practice) takes up between twenty and thirty-seven hours of the various programs.

With a system of recruitment that, as it were, presorts entrants to the police, the problem of providing induction training is much more complex than in the United States or Britain, where a single kind of training is given to ground recruits in their future work.

The *enquêteurs* receive the least training. A 164-hour program is designed to give them a picture of the police service, some acquaintance with penal law and procedure, with investigation and self-defense; they also receive instruction in typewriting, a skill they will need in the course of their duties. For those who will serve in certain branches, further programs are provided.

The *gardiens de la paix* receive six months' basic training, one month of which is spent on attachment to police formations. Their counterparts in New York City receive the same length of training, in London rather less. Three centers, at Reims, Châtelguyon, and Vannes, train those who will be posted to urban police in the provinces. A center at Vincennes prepares those who will serve in the Prefecture of Police of Paris. Recruits for the Republican Security Companies are trained at the CRS center at Sens.

The programs for the *gardiens de la paix* have a common grouping of subjects: General, Civic and Ethical; Specific Police Duties; Technical; Physical Education. The amount of time given to the subjects varies according to the missions for which the three categories of *gardiens* are being prepared.

The *officiers de paix* have a two-year program. It is important that those who will be the front-line leaders of the *gardiens de la paix* shall have a very good knowledge of the way the whole police system works and of its social implications, for it is "on the ground," where they and their subordinates provide a twenty-four-hour service, that the greatest proportion of police intervention and interaction with the public takes place. The *officier de paix* must appreciate the resources of the service and the way in which it will dispose of the patrol force's input. The two-year program is divided into twelve months at the *Ecole Supérieure des Officiers de Paix* at Nice, followed by a year of practical training in the operational sphere.

The *inspecteurs'* program lasts sixteen months. One month's pretraining is given, during which the candidate is assigned to observe in an urban police formation. This is followed by seven months' training at the *Ecole Nationale de Police* at Cannes-Ecluse, after which there are three months of initiation into practical plain clothes and uniform police work in a commissariat, a city detective department, and a regional crime service, participating actively in inquiries under the authority of an experienced *inspecteur*. Then comes a return to Cannes-Ecluse for two months of examinations, grading, and assignment, leading to first appointment, with confirmation a year later.

The training of the commissaires is rigorous and extensive in time and in subject matter. It is particularly associated with the *Ecole Nationale Supérieure de Police* at Saint-Cyr-au-Mont-d'Or. This establishment, classified as one of the *Grandes Ecoles* of France, is a focal point for the Police Nationale and its innumerable visitors from all over the world. Among its special features is its principal edifice, a handsomely austere building, formerly an Ursuline convent, set amid ample grounds on the heights overlooking the city of Lyon. Functional new buildings have been carefully sited to harmonize with the grounds and the old building. The *Ecole's* museum is very fine, with its unique Lacassagne and Locard criminalistics collections.

The commissaires' academic program, all of which is taken there, covers the whole spectrum of police work. The small permanent faculty of the school, all senior police officers, many of whom over the years have contributed memorably to the literature of the police and of the law, enjoy the ready cooperation of the Police Nationale's most important officials in their teaching. They also have the equally willing help of Prefects and Commissaires of the Republic, together with that of judges, prosecutors, *juges d'instruction,* officers of the Gendarmerie, civil administrators, medico-legists, and academics. Full use is made of the School's proximity to the world-famous University of Lyon.

The program begins on September 1st, when the student commissaires are initiated into the organization of the Ministry of the Interior and of the police services; they are assigned to their groups and meet their fellow students. Then follow eleven weeks of observation, nine of which are spent with an urban police formation (three weeks at the level of a *gardien de la paix,* one week at the level of an *inspecteur,* and three weeks at the level of a commissaire, then one week with General Intelligence, and one week with Criminal Investigation, in each case at *inspecteur* level). They write a paper on a set aspect of the role of the commissaire of police, which will be evaluated by the school's faculty. The next six months (December to June) are spent at the school, studying in the three academic departments of Human Sciences, General Police, and Criminal Police. There follow two and a half months at police training centers, where they study the role of a commissaire of police in the urban environment. A much-needed holiday is allowed at this point, after which they return to academic work at the school for the period September 15–December 1, with oral examinations. Six months of practical training ensue (December 1–June 1), including two and a half months with an urban police formation, a month of Criminal Investigation, a month of General Intelligence, a week with the Air and Frontier Police, a week with the CRS, two weeks with a private enterprise firm (where they gain insight into labor problems, useful in cases of conflict they may well encounter), and a week of initiation into work at a police training center, with a view to learning instructional skills. They then have the choice of spending a week in a prefecture, a prosecution department, a mayor's office, a Gendarmerie formation, or a prison. On June 1, they return to the *Ecole* for four weeks: a week of criticism of the system, two weeks of intensive oral examination by the faculty, when, inter alia, the candidate has to give a ten-minute talk on a subject allotted by chance, and to converse with the professorial board, and a week of interviews with directors of the central administration.

The graduation ceremonies are highly impressive and take place in the presence of the Minister of the Interior. At the final parade and march-past, when the new commissaires of police wear their silver-braided uniforms and tricolour sash for the first time, the Director of the school pronounces the formal address:

> Mesdames et Messieurs les Commissaires de Police, Monsieur le Ministre, Monsieur le Directeur-General and the High Personages accompanying them are about to present to you the tricolour sash which is the emblem of your dual quality as magistrate of the administrative and judicial order. May it always be for you the symbol of courage, civic spirit and abnegation.

THE JOB

The commissaires' first appointment will be to one of several posts. Aptitude and achievement at the College and on attachment will be the determining factors in deciding what the assignment will be. If the choice were left to the graduating class, most of them would probably opt for a post in the Urban Police, in the hope of being sent to take command of the police of a small city, where there would be a pleasant degree of independence. In Paris or other large cities, or in a headquarters branch, the newcomer takes a lowly place in a hierarchy. Least liked, it seems, are postings to General Intelligence, where much confinement to desk work will be hard to avoid. The other possibilities are Criminal Investigation, in Paris or one of the regional crime services, a Republican Security Company, Counter-Espionage, and the Air and Frontier Police.

Formality is very much more highly valued in France, the land that has been teaching manners to the civilized world since the seventeenth century, than it is in the United State or Britain. The new commissaire must observe a good deal of protocol. At Saint-Cyr-au-Mont-d'or there will have been full briefing on professional etiquette, of which the following may give some idea, though the amount of protocol varies in inverse proportion to the size of the organization to which the newcomer reports.

The first visit must be to the local chief of the police service and to one's colleagues, the introductions to the latter probably being effected by the chief. He will arrange for a visit to be paid to the Commissaire of the Republic of the Department, when it will also be wise to seek permission to call on the Commissaire's Secretary-General and other aides. A visit the same day must be paid to the Public Prosecutor and respects should be paid to the presiding judge of the senior trial court. Other judicial personages to be called upon include the judge of the Police Tribunal, in which court the commissaire may be required to represent the Public Prosecutor, and it is also as well to speak to the chief ushers of the local courts. At this stage, the Public Prosecutor will be arranging for the commissaire to be invested by the Prosecutor-General with the powers of an officer of judicial police. Nor are the municipal dignitaries to be overlooked. The mayor must certainly be visited and it is prudent to meet the mayoral aides. A visit to the commanding officer of the local Gendarmerie is essential and will show readiness to maintain good relations and to cooperate professionally. The military authorities should be called on, notably the general commanding. So, too, should local parliamentarians, irrespective of party, and a whole range of officials of the national civil service.

After the years of training and the initial courtesies of official life, the larger school of experience and responsibility begins its lessons. There may be spy catching, tackling terrorists at an airport, dealing with a difficult subordinate, equal or superior, confirming the facts in a case of adultery, interrogating a suspect in the *garde à vue,* evaluating the facts for an intelligence summary, discussing a strike with union leaders and management, interviewing complainants—anything, indeed, from contemplating the daily mountain of paperwork to standing where the missiles are flying, wearing the tricolour sash, calling out the classic warning, and ordering the CRS to charge.

Continuing the survey of job prospects after induction training, the *inspecteur,* who probably joined in hopes of becoming a detective, may be rewarded by assignment to an urban detective unit, a regional crime service, or the Criminal Investigation branch of the Prefecture of Police. It is quite likely, however, that the posting will be to General Intelligence, the Air and Frontier Police, or Counter-Espionage.

The *officer de paix* may go to the Prefecture of Police, in the capital's patrol force, or to a provincial police formation, or to the Air and Frontier Police, or to a Republican Security Company, where he will find himself addressed as *mon lieutenant,* in military style.

The *gardien de la paix* may go to the Prefecture of Police, to a provincial police formation, to the Air and Frontier Police, or to the CRS where he can serve until he is forty years of age, whereupon he will be transferred to the patrol branch of an urban police formation. It is likely, though, that before he reaches that age he will have found means to leave the Companies and exchange their barrack-based and mobile existence for duties less disruptive of family life.

The *enquêteur's* assignment will entail being a kind of minor *inspecteur,* a jack-of-all-trades at the call of the commissaire.

As regards promotion from the original grade, a commissaire may hope to be promoted to *commissaire principal* and then to *commissaire divisionnaire.* Beyond that lie the appointments of *contrôleur-général, inspecteur-général, sous-directeur,* and *directeur.* The *inspecteur's* next ranks are *inspecteur principal* and *inspecteur divisionnaire.* The *officier de paix* can rise to *officier de paix principal, commandant,* and *commandant de groupement.* The *gardien de la paix* can rise to *sous-brigadier, brigadier,* and *brigadier-chef.*

For uniformed personnel the retirement age is fifty-five, though officers in the *commandant* grades retire at fifty-six. The *inspecteur* grades retire at fifty-five. The commissaires and *commissaires principaux* retire at fifty-seven, *commissaires divisionnaires* at fifty-eight, and the higher grades at sixty.

Pension is granted on the basis of years of police service, which may be augmented by taking into consideration military or overseas service. The maximum pension, based on largest number of pensionable years, subject to a maximum of $37^1/_2$, is 75 percent of the highest salary the officer has earned. In certain cases forty years may be counted, yielding a pension of 80 percent of salary.

It is possible, as mentioned previously, for one to be promoted out of one's original corps, by undertaking the necessary studies and passing a competitive examination, or, in the case of promotion to the commissaire grade, in virtue of meritorious service. The Police Nationale makes correspondence courses and classes available.

FURTHER TRAINING

While the national police training system in France makes its major effort at the first formative stage on induction to the service, it does not neglect the need for further training in specialized fields and on promotion to new responsibilities. The British, who also have a national police training system (though not a national police), perhaps make more of an effort in further training, but any such disparity is largely due to the sketchiness of their basic programs. In the United States, police training at national level is provided on a limited scale by the Federal Bureau of Investigation of the U.S. Department of Justice and some "executive" development programs are offered by the International Association of Chiefs of Police and under the auspices of the Police Foundation of Washington, D.C. In the United States the predominant thrust is at the recruitment stage.

The Police Nationale's further training is systematic and still being developed. For the commissaire of police there are specialist courses on urban road traffic, maintenance of public order, fire prevention, and the protection and surveillance of juveniles. The *inspecteurs* have courses in accountancy, self-defense, photography, work with juveniles, policing of trade fairs, narcotics, communications, and there is a course for newly promoted *inspecteurs principaux.* The *officiers de paix* have a course to prepare them for instructional duties in training uniformed personnel and another course on the function and use of "intervention" companies (units of *gardiens de la paix,* raised from local police formations for purposes of public-order maintenance). The *gardiens de la paix* may be trained as physical education instructors, lifeguards, vehicle mechanics, radio telegraphists, dog handlers, mountain police, and typists.

A very important kind of further training is built into the French system. The in-service candidates for promotion to higher rank as *officier de paix, inspecteur,* and commissaire of police take the same substantial training programs as candidates admitted directly to those ranks from outside the service.

The Gendarmerie Nationale

A gendarme is a soldier but a soldier is not a gendarme. It is no easy task to make the change from a military to a police posture. It has nevertheless been done on innumerable occasions, with more or less success. But to make the change to the police role without forfeiting the military role is very much more difficult.

The Gendarmerie Nationale, premier regiment of the French Army, is also the most highly paid. Its dual charge amply justifies the difference in remuneration, for the gendarme, unlike other soldiers but like the civil police, is always on active service, year in, year out, providing a twenty-four-hour service to the community while at the same time being liable to turn from it to service on the battlefront.

The problem of making soldiers into gendarmes is tackled in France in many ways, but principally through the systems of recruitment and training. The Gendarmerie is fortunate in being able to attract a large enough number of good candidates for a high standard of selection to be maintained. Entry is at two levels, to the rank of gendarme (which since the eighteenth century has been rated as equivalent to that of a noncommissioned officer of cavalry) or to officer rank.

The applicant for training to become a gendarme must be French, have fulfilled his obligations to national service, be aged between eighteen and thirty-five years, at least 1 meter and 68 centimeters in height, in good health, and bear an impeccable character. No academic certificate is required. The admissions process is searching and thorough, more exacting than that of the civil police at a comparable level.

Once accepted, the recruit goes for a basic six-month course at one of the Gendarmerie's four recruit training centers, where the program includes military and physical education, police theory and practice, and, as with the Police Nationale's initial courses, general culture and ethics. Driving, typing, and first aid are also taught. After passing an examination at the end of the six months, the recruit becomes a gendarme-probationer and is sworn before a judge. The oath, as given in translation in Mr. J.R.J. Jammes's *Effective Policing,* is as follows: "I swear to obey my superior officers in all matters concerned with the service to which I am called and, in the execution of my duties, to use force solely for the maintenance of public order and for the enforcement of the law." Much of the secret of the successful formation of the gendarme undoubtedly lies in the formidable requirement of a four-year probationary stage, in which training continues and proofs of proficiency are exacted. Even the police of Japan, exigent as they are in their training, do not carry it so far. American, British, and French civil police devote comparatively little time to the early, crucial, basic training.

From the recruit center, though he may be posted to the Departmental Gendarmerie, the probationer usually goes to the Gendarmerie Mobile, where the largest single field will be in such police subjects as penal law and penal procedure, traffic control, and public order. Military training comes next in coverage, with general culture and physical education being pursued concurrently. A stiff examination awaits the probationers at the end of the two years, but success in this will qualify them for promotion to the higher noncommissioned ranks. They will be wise to take another examination that will enable them, when they have completed five years' service, to be empowered as officers of judicial police. On completion of the two years with the Gendarmerie Mobile the probationer may opt for further service there, or for transfer to the Departmental Gendarmerie or (if he meets the extra height requirement of an inch above the entrance standard) to the Republican Guard. He will continue training for another year.

Once sworn, of course, the gendarme can be employed on active police duties while his training is going on. The Republican Security Companies of the civil police do not keep their *gardiens* past the age of forty; the Gendarmerie ensures that no squadron of the Mobile Gendarmerie has more then 40 percent of its strength with more than eight to ten years' service; this is effected by transfers to the Departmental service.

As in the Police Nationale, the ambitious can study to earn advancement. Correspondence courses are available and courses are given by specialist centers. Promotion may be obtained up to the rank of sergeant-major, or one may qualify for training to become a commissioned officer. In these endeavors many succeed, a tribute to the soundness of both the selection and the training processes.

The officer corps is recruited from three categories: regular officers of the armed forces, reserve officers, and noncommissioned officers of the Gendarmerie. The selection process again is rigorous. The kind of training given is adjusted to the experience and qualifications, military and academic, of those admitted.

The training is given at the *Ecole des Officiers de la Gendarmerie Nationale* at Melun, one of France's *Grandes Ecoles*. For regular officers there is the one-year Higher Course, to which academically qualified reserve officers may also be admitted. Other reserve officers and noncommissioned officers of the Gendarmerie will take a one-year Preparatory Course, followed by a year on the Higher Course. Direct commissions in the rank of lieutenant may be granted to serving noncommissioned officers who are between forty and forty-six years of age with at least eighteen years' service. They are given a one-month course only. The Gendarmerie, no doubt in its wisdom, probably considers that there is not much more for such seasoned soldiers to learn.

Like that of the Police Nationale, the Gendarmerie's training system is hospitable to foreign countries, and the school at Melun opens a Preparatory Course to noncommissioned officers of foreign gendarmeries and the Higher Course to their officers. Preliminary training for the former is also given, for one year, at a preparatory center.

It is now possible for national military service to be satisfied by a year's service in the Auxiliary Gendarmerie. This consists of four months' training and eight months' service in an auxiliary and of course unsworn capacity with Gendarmerie units and formations.

The gendarme of Courteline's play would not, one feels, be quite at home in the Gendarmerie of the 1980s. The recruitment and training system of the Gendarmerie Nationale combines military and police science to generate professional excellence. It is a model of what can be achieved by training when government commits the necessary resources to it.

CHAPTER 10

Police and Criminal Justice

The Police Investigation

In the United States and Britain, all regular police officers have virtually the same powers with regard to criminal offenses, though in some instances police uniform must be worn. The patrol officer in the street, the detective in plain clothes, all officers, whatever their rank or specialism, have the same right to proceed in matters of crime.

It is not so in France. A *gardien de la paix* does not have the same powers as an *inspecteur,* nor does an *inspecteur* have the same powers as a commissaire of police. The Code of Penal Procedure, which in 1959 replaced (without greatly altering) Napoleon's Code of Criminal Instruction, distinguishes the categories of police powers.

First come the powers of those designated *officiers de police judiciaire,* officers of judicial police, familiarly known in France by the initials "OPJ" In this category are:

1. Mayors and Deputy Mayors. These elected officers, howev-

er, hardly ever have recourse to their powers in this respect and never initiate proceedings.

2. Officers and noncommissioned officers of the Gendarmerie and certain gendarmes of five or more years' service. Those serving in the Mobile Gendarmerie and the Republican Guard are excluded. It is not considered fitting for those on order-maintenance duties to exercise judicial powers.

3. Controllers-general, commissaires of police, *inspecteurs principaux,* and *inpecteurs divisionnaires* of the Police Nationale.

4. The Director and Deputy Directors of the Central Directorate of Criminal Investigation of the Police Nationale; the Director and Deputy Directors of the Gendarmerie.

Those in categories 2 and 3 above do not automatically have the right to exercise the powers of an officer of judicial police until they have been individually authorized to do so by the Prosecutor-General of the Court of Appeal of their jurisdiction. Those in categories 1 and 4 have such powers *ex officio.*

The powers in question include the right to impose the *garde à vue* on a suspected person. The term literally means "keep in sight" but in fact and in law involves being kept in police custody for twenty-four hours and, if the judicial authorities agree, for a further twenty-four hours. In narcotics cases the *garde à vue* may last for four days (twenty-four hours plus forty-eight hours plus twenty-four hours, the prolongations being authorized by the magistrate concerned after obligatory daily medical examinations). In cases concerning the security of the state, prolongation may be even more extensive, up to twelve days, but the law on this point is in process of being altered. Though the *garde à vue* is often attacked as a grave encroachment on the liberty of the individual, the police have so far managed to persuade the legislators that it is indispensable in the control of crime.

Another attribute of officers of judicial police is that they are entitled to sign the reports called *procès-verbaux.* The term needs a little explanation. Its literal meaning is "verbal proceedings," but the *procès-verbal* is always in written form. It is comforting to know that even in France it can be mystifying: it puzzles a young *inspecteur* in Willy-Paul Romain's novel, *L'Inspecteur en question,* who cannot see why it should be called verbal when it is in writing. A colleague enlightens him: during the Ancien Regime the lowly limbs of the law, their predecessors, were often illiterate and could only make their reports orally!

The next category consists of the *agents de police judiciaire,* "agents" as distinct from "officers" of judicial police. These are:

1. All gendarmes, except those classified as officers of judicial police; *inspecteurs* of the Police Nationale.
2. All members of the Police Nationale, except those classified as officers of judicial police; members of municipal police forces.

Those in category 1 are entitled to sign *procès-verbaux;* those in category 2 can only submit reports. The *procès-verbal,* as opposed to the report, is of high evidentiary value. No agent of the judicial police, of either category, has the power to order the *garde à vue.*

All crime discovered, by the police or anyone else, must be notified to the public prosecutor of the area. In most cases this is done in writing by the police; a serious case would be reported over the telephone. Once the prosecutor has been informed, the matter comes under his control and the police will act under his directions. This in some respects resembles the situation of the police and the district attorney in the United States, but differs totally from the procedure in England, where the decision to prosecute is in most instances taken by the police.

In France the activity of the police in criminal cases falls under three headings.

The first of these is the preliminary inquiry, a term that covers a whole complex of activities, involving the establishment of the fact that a crime has been committed, of its essential elements, the identification of the victim, witnesses, perpetrators, and accomplices—all that is done in the phase before the penal process proper begins in the hands of the *parquet,* the prosecutorial takeover. The prosecutor's office is known as the *parquet* from the days of the Ancien Regime, when the King's advocates had the right to stand and plead from the parquet flooring of the court: others had to stand on the stone flags bordering it. During the phase of the preliminary inquiry police may act on their own initiative or as directed by the public prosecutor. Police action may go as far as the detention of a suspect on police premises for the *garde à vue,* provided that this is imposed by an officer of judicial police. During the *garde à vue* the detainee has no right to see counsel or anyone else. A record is kept of rest allowed and meals provided and at the end of the period the person detained, or his relatives or friends, may require that he be examined by a medical doctor. There is no legal obligation to answer the questions of the police. If the detainee chooses to remain silent, that is his right. The fact that he said nothing, however, which is admissible in evidence in French court, will not be very helpful to his defense.

In the preliminary inquiry, an *inspecteur* may establish the case. Searches are allowed, with the suspect's permission; if this is refused, the public prosecutor is informed and will open a judicial inquiry; the *juge d'instruction* (see below) may then issue a search warrant or a rogatory commission.

The second kind of police activity in the criminal sphere concerns "flagrant" offenses, *crime flagrant* or *délit flagrant.* In the Latin of the Common Law, the term is *in flagrante delicto,* which, literally translated, means "while the crime is afire," but must be understood in the present context to mean while the crime is being committed or when the crime has been committed very recently. The "flagrancy" label in France applies only to offenses that are punishable by imprisonment. In flagrant offenses anyone can arrest the perpetrator but must bring him at once before the nearest officer of judicial police. At this point the arrested person is automatically placed in the *garde à vue* situation. Only officers of judicial police are competent to establish the case.

Flagrant offenses not only include offenses actually being committed or that have just been committed (as when someone is running from the scene of the crime, bloodstained or carrying stolen property) but also offenses when the suspect is being pursued by public outcry or is found in possession of objects likely to be the proceeds of the offense. In addition, where an officer of judicial police is asked by a head of household to see if an offense has been committed on his premises, the flagrancy classification applies.

A key question is for how long the state of flagrancy may continue. Authorities in France are at variance on the point. It has even been argued that once the police or judicial action begins, flagrancy ceases. Common sense, however, on the part of jurists (where it is not always in abundant supply) indicates some flexibility. The length of time during which an offense may be classed as flagrant may vary from a very short to a fairly lengthy period, but after thirty-six hours it is unlikely that an arrest without warrant would be sustained. The officer of judicial police, once informed of the offense, must notify the public prosecutor immediately and get on with the inquiry.

If the nature of the offense is such that it can be proved by seizing papers or other objects in the possession of those suspected of committing it, or of anyone else who might be holding them, the officer of judicial police goes to the domicile, makes a search and compiles a *procès-verbal;* the objects seized are placed under seal. Such searches cannot be made before 6.00 A.M. or after 9.00 P.M., except in special circumstances that are listed in the Code of Penal Procedure.

It is only in flagrant offenses that the police can arrest without warrant.

The third category of police activity in criminal cases is *en délégation judiciaire,* "in judicial delegation," when the police act as "delegates" of the public prosecutor or the *juge d'instruction,* who may give them warrants to search and seize, to arrest, or to summon witnesses, or they may issue a *commission rogatoire,* a rogatory commission, which is another kind of warrant, empowering the police to make general or particular inquiries in a case, or to question people either on specific points or with wider scope. Only officers of judicial police are qualified to act *en délégation judiciaire.* This third category of police action comes into operation once the public prosecutor or the *juge d'instruction* has taken charge.

The Magistracy

France's detectives, as mentioned on previous occasions, are regarded as "judicial" police because their action involves the judicial process and because, in the exercise of the investigative function, they are responsible to judicial authorities, in the first instance to the public prosecutor and at a later stage, in some cases, to the *juge d'instruction.* The status of officer of judicial police is conferred on individual officers by the Prosecutor-General of the Appeal Court of their jurisdiction, by whom it may be withdrawn, and it is he who writes an annual report on such officers. Thus, in criminal police work, the police, while remaining under the administrative authority of the Director-General of the Police Nationale, come under the authority of the magistracy. Similarly, the Gendarmerie, in such circumstances, remain under their Director-General and are controlled by the magistracy.

The French criminal justice system operates on the principle of the separation of powers. The organs of investigation are separated from the organs of prosecution, and both are separated from the organs of judgment. This is, perhaps, especially desirable by reason of the homogeneity of the criminal justice system in that nearly all of those who take part in its working, except lawyers in private practice and members of the public, are civil servants of the central government or members of its armed forces. There is no question whatever of elective office in the French system.

The magistracy in France, as in other European countries, does not consist only of the kind of persons who are called magistrates in the Anglo-American sense, meaning a judge of a trial court. In France it is understood, in the Roman sense, that a magistrate may be one of several kinds of senior officials in public service. The word is applied to judges, mayors, public prosecutors, *juges d'instruction,* certain Ministry of Justice officials, and commissaires and higher officers of the Police Nationale. The commissaire of police, indeed, is a very special official, a magistrate at once of the administrative and judicial orders.

The French distinguish between the *magistrat debout,* the magistrate on his feet, and the *magistrat de siege,* the seated magistrate, the judge in the Anglo-American sense.

Magistrates, with the exception of the police with magisterial status and the mayors, make their career within the structure of the Ministry of Justice. The entry point is now usually the National School of the Magistracy, founded in 1970, one of France's highest training establishments. Upon successful completion of the course, the new magistrate will probably start work as an assistant prosecutor, but in the course of his or her career may serve in various capacities: as an assessor (assistant judge), as the presiding judge of a court, as a prosecutor, as a ministry official, on a mission as observer or adviser on behalf of the government—or even as the Director-General of the Gendarmerie Nationale.

It is all very different from the Common Law's criminal justice administration. In the United States and in England, for instance, the judges are taken from advocates in private practice, experienced in the courts. The French would, no doubt, consider it ridiculous to expect an impartial judge to be conjured out of a lawyer who has spent his time taking one side or another in the trial situation. It seems only logical to them to train the judge as a judge, by years of service as an assessor. It can only be said that their system works. Visitors to French palaces of justice usually come away impressed by the competence of the judges. And French judges, civil servants though they are, are indomitably proud of their independence.

The Juge d'Instruction

There is no equivalent of the *juge d'instruction* in Common Law jurisprudence. Even to translate the term is difficult. Translators of novels and others usually settle for "examining magistrate," but that is a Common Law term of different significance; justices of the peace in England, for example, are called "examining justices" when they decide on whether there is a prima facie case to go for trial to a higher court, but this they do seated on the bench and in public. Literally, *juge d'instruction* means "judge of instruction," and it is from the literal meaning that the truth of the matter can best be reached. A judge, yes, but instruction? Instruction of whom? the answer to that is "the instruction of the trial court." What the *juge d'instruction,* heir of Louis XIV's *lieutenant-criminel de bailliage* and beyond him of the inquisitors of canon law, is required to do is to examine with a judicial eye the evidence that may lead to the trial of a serious offense. It is not, however, just a matter of scrutinizing evidence; it involves the direction of investigative work.

The corpus of knowledge for which he is responsible is embodied in the *dossier,* the case file, in which all the relevant information is assembled, and which, if the case goes for trial, will be placed in the hands of the presiding judge. The *juge d'instruction* must not be seen as an arm of the police or of the public prosecutor. As Professor A.E. Anton, who studied the subject at first hand, has written:

> The purely investigatory functions of the *juge d'instruction* could be taken over by the police; but the police are not quite free from the suspicion of being too anxious to secure convictions, and it is felt that investigation by a person of judicial status may shield innocent persons from the risk of being exposed to overzealous police interrogation. The device of *instruction* also ensures that an accused is not arraigned upon a serious charge in open court with all the attendant publicity unless and until a magistrate, after carefully and impartially investigating the facts, is prepared in effect to say that there is a sustainable case against him.

In the course of his inquiry, the *juge* will question the inculpated person, hear witnesses, collect background information, seek expert testimony and altogether assemble more comprehensive data than one would expect to find in the file of an American or a British case. The *juge* cannot, of course, do all the "leg work" necessitated by the scope of his inquiry. Though he may go to the scene of the crime, arrange reconstructions and leave his office for other purposes, the volume of business he has to transact usually confines him to his *cabinet.* Hence the delegation of officers of judicial police to carry out investigative work in his name and on his responsibility. Only he, however, is allowed to question the suspect once the case is in his charge.

When a suspect has been inculpated by the *juge* he has the right to counsel, at either his own or public expense. His counsel has the right to see whatever goes into the *dossier.* The proceedings take place in camera, protected by the law of professional secrecy, and were indeed secret until 1897, when counsel was allowed to the inculpated.

Criminal justice in France is often described as "inquisitorial," as opposed to the "accusatorial" procedure of the Common Law. The proceedings of the *juge d'instruction* are a perfect example of the inquisitorial system in principle and in practice.

When the inquiry is complete, the *dossier* will be sent to the public prosecutor with the *juge's* conclusion as to whether there is a case for trial or not. If the prosecutor agrees that there is, after several formal exchanges, the *dossier* will be considered by the Chamber of Accusation and sent to the trial court.

The system of the *juge d'instruction* is not without drawbacks, the main one being the amount of time it takes to complete a case. It will be many months before the trial takes place and it is possible for an inculpated person to be kept in preventive detention for the whole period between inculpation and being tried. The *juge's* task is immensely complicated by the number of cases to be dealt with, sometimes approaching two hundred in one year, several of which are probably being dealt with concurrently. French critics of the system also say that the independence of the *juge d'instruction* is seriously compromised by the extent to which he has in practice to rely on the police.

The great majority of criminal cases do not involve the *juge d'instruction*. Only in the more serious or complicated cases does the public prosecutor ask for his services. The much more common procedure is for the public prosecutor to act on the results of the police inquiries.

France distinguishes three categories of criminal offense. The first is the *crime,* approximately equivalent to the American felony. In all cases of *crime* the *juge d'instruction* is brought in. The second is the *délit,* the delict, akin to the American misdemeanor, in some cases of which, as when the perpetrator is unknown or the suspect has a bad record, the *juge d'instruction* may be required to act. The third category, the *contravention,* akin to the American violation, does not require the *juge d'instruction's* services. *Crimes* are tried in the Assize Court; *délits* in the Correctional Tribunal; *contraventions* in the Police Tribunal.

The Criminal Justice System in Operation

It may be helpful to trace some of the stages through which a serious criminal offense passes, as so far the criminal justice system has been considered abstractly.

A man commits an armed robbery in a quiet city street, taking a wallet from the victim, whom he stabs. He is seen by two people as he makes his escape. They call a *gardien de la paix,* who gives first aid and calls an ambulance to take the wounded man to hospital. He then telephones the officer of judicial police at his commissariat.

The OPJ calls the public prosecutor and gets on with inquiries. These produce good descriptions of the robber and his weapon, with details of the wallet and its contents supplied from his hospital bed by the victim. All this is recorded in *procès-verbaux.* The description fits a man already suspected of similar offenses in the same neighborhood. A watch is kept on his usual haunts and he is arrested two hours later with the wallet and knife in his possession. The arrest was justified in being made without warrant because the offense was flagrant.

On arrival at the commissariat, the perpetrator is automatically placed in the *garde à vue* situation, by reason of the seriousness of the offense: it ranks as a *crime.* During the twenty-four hours of the *garde à vue* the detainee, as the law requires, is given meals and allowed to rest in the intervals of interrogation. This is recorded in detail. He says very little. The OPJ informs the Public Prosecutor and applies for a prolongation of the *garde à vue,* which is granted. Further interrogation results in a statement, amounting to a confession, which is recorded in a *procès-verbal.* The OPJ, after informing him of his right to ask for a medical examination, takes the suspect to the Public Prosecutor, who then opens an *information,* formal legal proceedings, and a *juge d'instruction* is designated, before whom the prisoner is now taken.

At this first meeting, *Monsieur* (or perhaps *Madame) le juge* establishes the suspect's identity and social status, then informs him that he has been "inculpated" (the word "accused" will not be used until after the *instruction* is complete) for the offense he is said to have committed. The judge tells him that he is not obliged to say anything and that he has the right to demand that he shall not be interrogated save in the presence of counsel, whom he is at liberty to choose (legal aid is publicly provided in appropriate instances). Then, in view of the violence used against the victim he orders the suspect into preventive detention. There, unless his appeals for provisional liberty are allowed, which is unlikely in such a case, he will remain until the case is disposed of.

Some days later, the judge sees him again, this time in the presence of counsel, who has, as the law requires, been given access to all the documentation on file in the judge's dossier. The inculpated now retracts his confession, alleging that the police forced it from him by brutality. It is, he says, a case of mistaken identity. He had found the wallet and knife in the street some time after the crime. While it was being committed he was with a girlfriend.

All these matters are duly recorded, the judge's clerk taking them down in the form of *procès-verbaux.* The judge issues rogatory commissions to the police so that inquiries can be made into them, and also so that other information can be sought, notably on the lifestyle and background of the inculpated. The judge also requires scientific testimony on the wound and the weapon. The victim, now convalescent, and the witnesses are brought to the judge's chambers for confrontation with the inculpated. The complaint of police brutality raises the question of why a medical examination was not requested at the end of the *garde à vue* and an examination now ordered by the judge produces no evidence to support the allegation.

The pressure of other business and the time taken for the police inquiries (which nullify the alibi defense as the lady in question cannot substantiate it) prevent the judge from completing the process of *information,* probably for some months. If it passes the four-month mark, the judge will renew his order for preventive detention for another four-month period, which with luck will suffice. If not, he can always renew it for another four months. Once he has finished his inquiries, the judge will send the *dossier* to the public prosecutor. When any questions the latter may raise have been settled, the *dossier* goes to the Chamber of Accusation where it is thoroughly examined by a *rapporteur* and three judges, who may require further questions to be settled. Once they find it in order, it is sent to the Assize Court. The *instruction* is over and the judge who has conducted it takes no further part whatever in the proceedings.

The inculpated, who has now become the accused, will be tried by jury. Only in the Assize Court does a jury sit in France; in the other courts judgment is entirely a matter for judges. There are only about 1,500 jury trials a year; there is an Assize Court in each department, sitting quarterly. It is common practice for a charge to be reduced if a guilty plea is indicated, so that, for instance, the "armed" element will be deleted from an armed robbery charge;

154

the case can then be dealt with by the next lower court, the Correctional Tribunal. Similarly, the element of "indecency" might be deleted from a charge of indecent assault, so that the case will be triable in the court next lower from the Correctional Tribunal, the Police Tribunal. Plea bargaining is by no means an exclusively American phenomenon.

French court procedure, like English, is much more formal than court procedure in the United States. In the criminal courts the judges wear red robes, as does the public prosecutor. The frequent interruptions by counsel, commonplace in America, would not be tolerated by any French tribunal. Conversely, the laws of evidence are much less restrictive and the previous convictions of the accused are made known during the hearing.

To the presiding judge falls the orchestration of the trial. The two assessors, seated on either side of him (or her), rarely intervene. The jury is chosen by lot from those summoned for the occasion. The business of *voir dire*, which consumes so much time in the United States, is soon despatched in France, the public prosecutor being allowed four challenges and the defense five.

When the act of accusation has been read by the clerk of the court, the presiding judge (not the public prosecutor) questions the accused and leads the evidence. The witnesses are called in whatever order the judge decides. Prosecutor and defense counsel cross-examine as and when the judge allows. When the evidence has been heard, the public prosecutor makes a speech, probably stressing the heinousness of the offense and the social desirability of making an example of the offender, and demands the sentence the prosecution considers appropriate. It is now the turn of the defense counsel to do what he can for his client, which is often an opportunity for impassioned and stylish eloquence. The accused is then given an opportunity to make a statement to the court.

The judge reads out the points on which the jurors have to decide and gives the classic caution that it is essential for the juror to have a *conviction intime*, an inner conviction, of the guilt of the accused if a guilty verdict is to be given.

The jury retires to consider its verdict. Its nine lay members are now augmented by three professional ones, as the judge and the two assessors retire to deliberate and vote with them. This practice is often criticized in France; many people think that the judge and his two colleagues must carry undue weight. A majority verdict of eight suffices for conviction.

The notion, prevalent in the United States and in Britain, that in France an accused person has to prove innocence, while in Anglo-American law guilt has to be proved by the prosecution, is indignantly contradicted by French jurists. The onus, as they emphasize, is on the prosecution to prove guilt in open court. If the dice seem loaded against the accused, as when the presiding judge leads the evidence, it should be remembered that the inculpated person has had every opportunity—and no such opportunity of the same nature exists in Common Law criminal procedure—to be exculpated during the inquisitorial examination of the affair by the *juge d'instruction* in the presence of defense counsel.

Interpol

France has been prominent from the outset in the promotion of international criminal police work. When the idea of international cooperation in this sphere was first propounded in Europe at a conference of jurists, police, and criminologists at Monte Carlo in 1914, the prime movers included serving and former senior officers of the Prefecture of Police and the *Sûreté Générale.* The First World War postponed action and it was not until 1923, mainly at Austrian instigation, that the International Criminal Police Commission was established, with headquarters in Vienna. The Second World War brought the suspension of the commission's activities, no meetings of the members being held after the Nazis moved into Austria in 1938, whereafter the Third Reich took charge of the archives.

In 1946 international police cooperation entered upon its modern phase with the reconstitution of the commission. As its headquarters could not be relocated in Vienna, then under four-power Allied control, a new home had to be found. The French government offered a building in Paris, which was accepted, and the first Secretary-General, the organization's chief executive, was Louis Ducloux, head of the criminal investigation branch of the

Sûreté Nationale, with Jean Népote, a young but also senior officer of the *Sûreté,* as his deputy. Monsieur Népote was to serve as deputy to Ducloux's successor, Marcel Sicot, before himself becoming Secretary-General in 1963, holding this office for over a decade.

Jean Népote thus gave the executive direction of the modern Interpol invaluable continuity for over thirty years. It is one of the rare instances of a man who held police office for a long time without overstaying his usefulness. It is to his powers of organization, his consummate diplomacy, and his personal high standing with the member nations that Interpol's development to its present status is due. His successor, another senior French police officer, continues France's sterling contribution to international criminal policing.

Interpol is not, as many people imagine, a force of international detectives with worldwide jurisdiction. It is an international clearinghouse and data bank for the member nations. In each country there is one National Central Bureau that transmits and receives on behalf of all that country's criminal police agencies information by direct link to Interpol's headquarters, now at Saint-Cloud, near Paris. Thus, if the New York City Police Department, the Michigan State Police, or any other regular law-enforcement agency, large or small, in the United States, needs to receive or transmit data on some crime or criminal, it communicates with Interpol headquarters through the National Central Bureau in the U.S. Department of Justice in Washington, D.C. In Britain, whichever police force needs this service goes through the National Central Bureau at New Scotland Yard.

In France the Director-General of the Police Nationale is the chief of the National Central Bureau, the office of which is at his headquarters in the rue des Saussaies. Through this office the Gendarmerie and the various branches of the Police Nationale communicate with Interpol headquarters, following the same procedure as the other member nations.

Though the Secretaries-General of Interpol have all been French, the Secretariat-General has recruited its staff increasingly from other nations, resulting in the very representative personnel who constitute the headquarters staff today.

Epilogue

THE POLICE OF FRANCE have probably existed as a professional body longer than any other police in Europe. They differ markedly from such latecomers to the professional police scene as their counterparts in the United States and Britain, not least in the length and continuity of their development. The *commissaires-enquêteurs au Châtelet* and the *prévôts* of the *maréchaussée* are unmistakably the ancestors of the modern commissaires of police and the officers of the Gendarmerie, and both go back to the Middle Ages. Royal officials then, republican officials today, they stand for the authority of the state of France in a way that no police official in America or Britain stands for the federal or national governance of the two countries. The evolution of the French police is an inseparable process in the evolution of the French state.

Relatively more powerful in terms of numbers, the French police are also more powerful in terms of law. They nevertheless resemble the American and British police in being under the rule of law and in ultimate answerability to law and to a democratically elected legislature. The law in question, of course, is of a different juridical family, belonging to the Roman and not to the Common Law tradition.

Another obvious difference lies in the duality of their system, its age-old reliance upon two sharply distinct kinds of police, one military, the other civil, and in those two kinds being aggregated in monolithic form, directly dependent on ministries and bureaucracies of the central government.

Yet similarities assert themselves even more markedly. There are main objectives in common: the basic purposes of the prevention and detection of crime, the protection of life and property, the preservation of public tranquillity. The main technique of enforcement is common: the uniformed patrol manifesting the presence of the police. So is the use of technological resources. Common, too, is the problem of crime, for the growth of criminality in France follows the unhappy pattern of its growth in almost all advanced societies. Durkheim noted in 1893 that "it has increased everywhere," and crime figures have gone on increasing in a way that Professor Sir Leon Radzinowicz has described as "grim and relentless in their ascending monotony." France has problems of organized crime, of crimes against persons and property, of juvenile delinquency, narcotics and terrorism, and to each new challenge the response, as elsewhere, has been to create specialist branches and units. French firearms regulations were made stricter in the late 1950s but arms are still widespread among the population. Over thirty police and gendarmes may be killed in the course of a year; in the United States, with four and a half times the population, the figure is approximately one hundred; in England and Wales the total number of officers killed since 1900 is seventy-two.

All uniformed police in France routinely carry firearms. A civil police officer may use arms on individual initiative in legitimate self-defense and when there is no other means of defending a position the officer has been ordered to hold. The use of arms by a police formation is legal only when the order to fire has been given by the officer in command, and that order can only be given after a prescribed series of verbal warnings and announcements (to which attention must be drawn by drum beat, trumpet call, red rocket, or red torch flashes) by an officer wearing the tricolor emblem of the magistracy, normally a commissaire of police.

The Gendarmerie are subject to the same control in the collective use of arms, save that they may be used to defend persons entrusted to them and when resistance cannot be overcome by any other means. In the use of arms on individual initiative, however, the Gendarmerie have much greater scope. A gendarme may use arms against:

- armed persons who are threatening him;
- persons trying to escape from his custody or his inquiries, after due warning;
- drivers of vehicles who do not obey his order to stop, after due warning.

It would seem that the military police's wider charter in the matter of arms has led to the Gendarmerie rather than the Police Nationale incurring the censure of contemporary writers. Denis Langlois devotes a chapter to the abuse of arms in his book *Les Dossiers Noirs de la Police Française* in which the principal incidents discussed concern gendarmes.

Complaints of police brutality are not uncommon in France. To what extent they are justified, or to what extent police brutality is condoned, is another matter. In confrontations of turbulent crowds and police formations it is always to be expected that in any country where there is a free press the police will be accused either of undue violence or insufficient firmness. It is more disturbing, however, to find that violence against persons in custody is part of the public's traditional perception of the police. In modern times, the police have been hard on offenders within their own ranks and the criminal courts have seen not a few prosecutions of police officers. Police union leaders have spoken out strongly against unnecessary use of force.

As in the United States and Britain, there is considerable unionization of the police (though not of the Gendarmerie, by reason of its military character). There are indeed official representative organs of each of the corps of police officials as well as associations on trade union lines. There are not as many of the latter as there are in the United States, with its more than 25,000 police agencies, but more than there are in England, where a single professional association represents all ranks up to chief inspector and two others look after the superintendents and chief officers. In none of the three countries do police have the right to strike, though they lost it in France as recently as 1948. David Watts

Pope, writing on August 27, 1982, in *Police Review*, comments that as French police may also join nonpolice unions there is consequently a greater political awareness on their part; he remarks that the police unions there enjoy more consultation than in Britain. There is good evidence that their union leaders, like their British counterparts, are out for more than material benefits for their members; they campaign also for better training and higher standards of recruitment. Gérard Monate's *Questions à la Police* reflects a genuinely enlightened view of police affairs; at the time when the book was published Monate was Secretary-General of the *Fédération autonome des Syndicats de Police,* the most important of the police unions.

Monsieur Monate, like other recent police authors, places great emphasis on the concept of the police officer as citizen and the need for a more open style of policing. He denounces the kind of illegalities that the authorities commit in their endless quest for information—wire taps, interception of mail, secret compilation of files on people, surveillance by shadowing—and deplores the damage done to the police in the eyes of the public by being involved in such practices. He finds interference with civil liberty is all too frequent: inability to produce proof of one's identity, for instance, if a police officer demands it, leads automatically to being taken to a police station to have it established. The public does not like such procedures but seems to have come to tolerate them. "Is there anything more respectable than an ancient abuse?" asks a character in Voltaire's *Zadig* (to be told: "Reason is more ancient").

A French magistrate, many years ago, during the Fourth Republic, said to the present writer, "We are a police state." Jack Hayward, in *The One and Indivisible French Republic,* comments:

> Because of the extensive prerogative police power that exists in France and the latitude accorded to the police force in exercising these powers, of all the liberal democratic countries the French police system would most effortlessly fit into a totalitarian form of government which the fear of revolution and civil war might bring about.

The police in France, as we have seen, have grown along with the country's whole political evolution, as part of that complex accumulation and concentration of power by the state as it has moved to present times by way of monarchies, empires, revolutions, republics, and wars. In this process police have come to notice more than they have in America or Britain and been subjected to far more general examination and scrutiny. What national figures in either of those countries are associated with police development? Robert Peel, of course, for his foundation of the Metropolitan Police of London; Theodore Roosevelt, maybe, for his brief police commissionership in New York City; Winston Churchill, perhaps, who secured a weekly rest day for the service when he was Home Secretary! France has a different tale to tell. The greatest names of her history are writ large in police annals: Louis XIV, Napoleon, Clemenceau, de Gaulle. When police systems are largely of local provenance, as they are in the United States and Britain, historians pay little attention to them. No one wrote a general history of the British police service until Melville Lee showed the way in 1900; general histories of the American police have only begun to be written since the Second World War. France, on the other hand, has a grand array of police literature, from the four stately volumes of Nicolas de La Mare's eighteenth-century *Traité de la Police* to the beautiful books of the *Encyclopédie Nationale de Police* and *Huit Siècles de Gendarmerie* of our own time. There is no getting away from the fact that police is more important in France than it is across the Channel or across the Atlantic.

This is surely because in France the state as well as the citizen has to look to the police for protection. A special relationship in consequence exists between police and government. Casamayor, unyielding and eloquent critic of institutions, says in his book *La Police* that it is government policy to rule the police by dividing it into several distinct hierarchies, corps, and specializations and also by encouraging the unpopularity of the service: the state's great secret hold on the police is to appear to be the police's only friend! The police do not much relish being cast in this role, as became evident one memorable day* when they came forth from their stations into the streets and talked to the public about the service they are there to give them. It is only fair to Casamayor to recall that he also believes that of all the public services, the police have the best chance of staying in touch with reality, for—and here the

*March 4, 1971.

basic similarity of police forces comes in—to the police officer the job always comes first and the job is inseparable from people and from the hard discipline of fact. And Casamayor pleads for a more open style of policing, for information without delation, discretion without mystery, for a police that has melted into the human community. That he and many others have felt free to write so frankly about France's police and criminal justice system is perhaps hardly evidence in favor of the totalitarian prospect envisaged by Mr. Hayward.

The part of the police in France's remarkable political, social, and economic recovery since the Second World War has been far greater than radical critics are ever likely to concede. The adverse factors militating against that recovery were many and powerful: the traumas left by defeat and occupation, by the disruption and loss of overseas sovereignty, by the fierce fermentation of civil strife. That order was restored in times of crisis and maintained overall during a sorely troubled epoch is proof enough of the strength and resilience of France's police systems. The stability of France today owes a great deal, unquantifiable as such debts are, to the internal defenses that stood the test against forces which, had they not been stoutly resisted, would have destroyed the Republic.

Nations carve their police systems in their own likeness. The police style of London would not be effective in New York, any more than the style of New York would be effective in London. Neither would be effective in Paris. The present account has sought to be objective in tracing the growth of one of the world's major and most influential police models. That model differs from American and British models in the balance of its activities, devoting much more time to information-intelligence functions and holding very much more strength in order-maintenance reserve. But it all comes down in the end to the basic police duties in the community. Anyone with any considerable experience of the French police, civil or military, is well aware of high quality in personnel and performance.

Bibliography

ABRAHAM, HENRY J. *The Judicial Process: An Introductory Analysis of the Courts of the United States, England and France.* 3rd ed. New York: Oxford University Press, 1975.

ANGELI, CLAUDE. *See* Backmann, René.

ANTON, A.E. "L'Instruction Criminelle," *American Journal of Comparative Law,* 9, no. 3, (Summer 1960).

ARON, RAYMOND. *La Revolution Introuvable: Reflexions sur la Revolution de Mai.* Paris: Fayard, 1968.

ARRIGHI, JEAN-PIERRE, and ASSO, BERNARD. *La Police Nationale: Missions et Structures.* Paris: Editions de la Revue Mondaine, 1979.

ASSO, BERNARD. "Police Nationale et Police Municipale," *Police Nationale,* 99, 100 (1976): 23–25, 13–23. 1976.

BACKMANN, RENÉ, and ANGELI, CLAUDE. *Les Polices de la Nouvelle Société.* Paris: François Maspero, 1971.

BECKER, HAROLD K. *Police Systems of Europe.* Springfield, Ill.: Charles C. Thomas, 1973.

BELIN, JEAN. *My Work at the Sûreté.* Trans. Eric Whelpton. London: George C. Harrap, 1950.

BOUCLY, JACQUES, and LE CLÈRE, MARCEL. *Code de Procédure Pénale Commenté.* Paris: Editions Police-Revue, 1973.

164

BUISSON, HENRY. *La Police, Son Histoire.* Paris: Nouvelles Editions Latines, 1958.

———*Fouché, Duc D'Otrante.* Bienne, Switzerland: Editions du Panorama, 1968.

BURNAT, ANDRE. *La Brigade des Moeurs: Les Inspecteurs Racontent.* Paris: Presses de la Cite, 1975.

CANLER, LOUIS. *Mémoires de Canler: Ancien Chef du Service de Sûreté.* Ed. Jacques Brenner. Paris: Mercure de France, 1968.

CARR, JOHN. *The Stranger in France: or, a Tour from Devonshire to Paris.* London: 1803.

CASAMAYOR. *Le Bras Séculier: Justice et Police.* Paris: Editions du Seuil, 1960.

———*La Police.* Paris: Gallimard, 1973.

CATHALA, FERNAND. *Cette Police Se Decriée.* Saverdun: Editions du Champ-de-Mars, 1971.

——— *Pratiques et Réactions Policières.* Saverdun: Editions du Champ-de-Mars, 1977.

CHABANNES, JACQUES. *Les Scandales de la "Troisiéme."* Paris: Librairie Académique Perrin, 1972.

CHAPMAN, BRIAN: *The Prefects of Provincial France.* London: Allen and Unwin, 1955.

——— *Police State.* London: Pall Mall Press, 1970.

CHASSAIGNE, MARC. *La Lieutenance Générale de Police de Paris.* Geneva: Slatkine Megariotis Reprints, 1975.

CLAUDE. *Mémoires de Monsieur Claude: Chef de la Police de Sûreté sous le Second Empire. 18e Ed.* 7 vols. Paris: Jules Rouff, 1881.

COATMAN, JOHN. *Police.* London: Oxford University Press, 1959.

COBB, RICHARD. *The Police and the People: French Popular Protest 1789–1820.* Oxford: Oxford University Press, 1970.

——— *Reactions to the French Revolution.* London: Oxford University Press, 1972.

——— *Paris and its Provinces: 1792–1802.* London: Oxford University Press, 1975.

Code Pénal. 71e Ed. Paris: Dalloz, 1973–1974.

Code de Procédure Pénale. 15e Ed. Paris: Dalloz, 1973–1974.

COURTELINE. *Le Gendarme est sans Pitié.* Paris: Flammarion, 1974.

CRAMER, JAMES. *The World's Police.* London: Cassell, 1964.

DÉMARET, PIERRE, and PLUME, CHRISTIAN. *Target de Gaulle.* Trans. Richard Barry. New York: Dial Press, 1975.

DENIS, GUY. *Citoyen Policier.* Paris: Albin Michel, 1976.

———— *L'Enquête Préliminaire: Etude Théorique et Pratique*. Paris: Editions Police-Revue, 1974.

D'HAUTERIVE, ERNEST. *La Police Secreté du Premier Empire: Bulletins Quotidiens Adressés par Fouché à l'Empéreur*. Vols I–III. Paris: Librairie Académique Perrin, 1913; Vols IV, V, Paris: Librairie P. Clavreuil, 1963, 1964.

DILNOT, GEORGE (ED.). *The Trial of the Detectives*. London: Bles, 1928.

DIRAND, GEORGES, and JOLY, PIERRE. *Maître, Vous Avez la Parôle: René Floriot, Raymond Filippi, Joannès Ambre*. Paris: Calmann-Lévy, 1975.

DUCLOUX, LOUIS. *From Blackmail to Treason: Political Crime and Corruption in France 1920–40*. Trans. Ronald Matthews. London: Andre Deutsch, 1958.

DUPEUX, GEORGES. *La France de 1945 à 1969*. 3rd ed. Paris: Librairie Armand Colin, 1972.

DURIN, LUCIEN. *Autopsie d'une Singulière Affaire Criminelle*. Paris: Nouvelles Editions Baudiniere, 1980.

DURKHEIM, EMIL. *Les Règles de la Méthode*. Paris: 1893.

EDWARDS, STEWARD. *The Paris Commune 1871*. London: Eyre and Spottiswoode, 1971.

FLORIOT, RENÉ. *When Justice Falters*. Trans. and ed. by Rayner Heppenstall. London: Harrap, 1972.

FORSTENZER, THOMAS R. *French Provincial Police and the Fall of the Second Republic: Social Fear and Counterrevolution*. Princeton, N.J.: Princeton University Press, 1981.

FOSDICK, RAYMOND B. *European Police Systems* (1915). Montclair, N.J.: Patterson Smith, 1969.

FOUCHÉ, JOSEPH. *Memoires de Joseph Fouché, Duc d'Otrante: Ministre de la Police Générale*. 2nd ed. Paris: Le Rouge, 1824.

FOUCHET, CHRISTIAN. *Mémoires d'Hier et de Demain: Au Service du General de Gaulle. Londres 1940, Varsovie 1945, Alger 1962, Mai 1968*. Paris: Plon, 1971.

FUNCK-BRENTANO, FRANTZ. *Le Drame des Poisons*. 13th ed. Paris: Librairie Hachette, 1920.

GAYET, JEAN. *ABC de Police Scientifique*. Paris: Payot, 1973.

GÉVRAUDAN, HONORÉ. *Tiens, vous faîtes ce métier la!* Paris: Fayard, 1974.

GLUECK, SHELDON. *Continental Police Practice: In the Formative Years*. A Report made in 1926 to Colonel Arthur Woods, the Police Commissioner of the City of New York. Springfield, Ill. Charles C. Thomas, 1974.

GORON, M. *Les Mémoires de M. Goron.* 4 vol. Paris: Flammarion, n.d.

GRIMAUD, MAURICE. *En Mai Fais ce qu'il te Plaît.* Paris: Stock, 1977.

GROUSSARD, GEORGES A. *Chemins secrets.* Tome I. Mulhouse, Paris, Lausanne: Bader-Dufour, 1948.

————*Service secret 1940–1945.* Paris: La Table Ronde, 1964.

GUYOT, YVES. *La Police.* Paris, 1884.

HAYWARD, JACK. *The One and Indivisible French Republic.* London: Weidenfeld and Nicolson, 1973.

HEAD, SIR FRANCIS. *A Faggot of French Sticks; or, Paris in 1851.* New York: George P. Putnam, 1852.

Huit Siècles de Gendarmerie. Toulouse–Paris: Editions Larrieu-Bonnel, 1967.

JAMMES, J.R.J. *Effective Policing: The French Gendarmerie.* Bradford, England: M.C.B. Publications, 1982.

JOLY, PIERRE. *See* Dirand, Georges.

Le Journal Officiel de la République Française. Débats Parlementaires. Assemblée Nationale. Mercredi 22 juin 1966.

KING, JOAN. *See* Radzinowicz, Sir Leon.

LABORDE, JEAN. *The Dominici Affair.* Trans. Milton Waldman. London: Collins, 1974.

LAMBERT, LOUIS. *Formulaire des Officiers de Police Judiciaire.* Paris: Editions Police-Revue, 1970.

LANGLOIS, DENIS. *Les Dossiers Noirs de la Police Française.* Paris: Editions du Seuil, 1971.

LANTIER, JACQUES. *Le Temps des Policiers: Trente Ans d'Abus.* Paris: Fayard, 1970.

LARGUIER, JEAN. *La Procédure Penale.* Paris: Presses Universitaires de France, 1963.

LAROCHE-FLAVIN, CHARLES. *La Machine Judiciaire.* Paris: Editions du Seuil, 1968.

LARRIEU, GÉNÉRAL. *Histoire de la Gendarmerie: Depuis les origines de la maréchaussée jusqu'à nos jours.* Paris, 1921.

LARUE, ANDRÉ. *Les Flics.* Paris: Fayard, 1969

LE CLÈRE, MARCEL. *Histoire de la Police.* Paris: Presses Universitaires de France, 1973.

———— *Le 6 février.* Paris: Hachette, 1967.

———— *La Police.* Paris: Presses Universitaires de France, 1972.

———— *Manuel de Police Technique.* 2nd ed. Paris: Editions Police-Revue, 1974.

LENIN, V.I. *See* Marx, Karl.

Liaisons. Revue d'information et de relations publiques éditée par la préfecture de police. Paris: 1963–.

MACÉ, G. *Le Service de Sûreté*. Paris: 1885.

MADELIN, LOUIS. *Fouché. 1759–1820*. Paris: Plon, 1900.
———*Fouché. 1759–1820*. Paris: Plon, 1955.

MANCEAU, MICHELE. *Les Policiers Parlent*. Paris: Editions du Seuil, 1969.

MARCELLIN, RAYMOND. *L'Ordre public et les groupes révolutionnaires*. Paris: Plon, 1969.

MARX, KARL. *The 18th Brumaire of Louis Bonaparte*. New York: International Publishers, 1975.
———and LENIN, V.I. *The Paris Commune*. New York: International Publishers, 1968.

MONATE, GERARD. *Questions à la Police*. Paris: Stock, 1974.

MONTALDO, JEAN. *Les Corrompus, avec un Chapitre Inedit*. Paris: La Table Ronde, 1971.

MONTREUIL, JEAN. *See* Parra, Charles
———*See* Ravier, Paul.

MOSSIKER, FRANCES. *The Affair of the Poisons*. New York: Alfred A. Knopf, 1969.

NATIONAL ADVISORY COMMISSION ON HIGHER EDUCATION FOR POLICE OFFICERS. *See* Sherman, Lawrence W.

PAILLOLE, PAUL. *Services Spéciaux 1935–1945*. Paris: Editions Robert Laffont, 1975.

PARRA, CHARLES, and MONTREUIL, JEAN. *Traité de Procédure Pénale Policière*. Paris: Quillet, 1970.

PLUME, CHRISTIAN. *See* Démaret, Pierre.

Police. Monthly Magazine of the Police Federation of England and Wales. 1966–.

Police Journal. Quarterly. Chichester, England: Barry Rose, 1928–.

Police Nationale. Paris: 1968–.

Police Review. Weekly. London: 1882–.

Police Studies. Quarterly. London and New York: 1978–.

RADZINOWICZ, SIR LEON. *Ideology and Crime: A Study of Crime in Its Social and Historical Context*. London: Heinemann, 1966.
———and King, Joan, *The Growth of Crime: The International Experience*. London: Hamish Hamilton, 1977.

RAISSON, HORACE. *Histoire de la Police de Paris: 1667–1844.* Paris: A. Levavasseur, 1844.

RAVIER, PAUL, AND MONTREUIL, JEAN. *L'Enquête de Police Judiciaire.* Limoges–Paris: Lavavazelle, 1979.

Revue de la Sûreté Nationale. Paris: 1957–1968.

REY, ALFRED, and FÉRON, LOUIS. *Histoire du Corps des Gardiens de la Paix.* Paris: Librairie de Firmin-Didot, 1896.

RHODES, HENRY T.F. *Alphonse Bertillon: Father of Scientific Detection.* London: George G. Harrap, 1956.

ROCHES, ANDRÉ (ED.). *Encyclopédie Nationale de la Police.* Paris: Compagnie Nationale de Diffusion du Livre, 1955.

ROMAIN, WILLY-PAUL. *Le Dossier de la Police: En Bourgeois et en Tenue.* Paris: Librairie Académique Perrin, 1966.

———*L'Inspecteur en Question.* Paris: La Table Ronde, 1962.

———*Les Commissaires.* Paris: Presses de la Cité, 1963.

ROMEU, A. *Le Juge d'instruction.* Angoulême: Imprimerie Générale Charentaise, 1975.

SARAZIN, JAMES. *La Police en Miettes: Le Systeme Marcellin.* Paris: Calmann-Levy, 1974.

SAVANT, JEAN. *La Vie Fabuleuse et Authentique de Vidocq.* Paris: Editions du Seuil, 1950.

SCHNAPP, ALAIN, AND VIDAL-NAQUET, PIERRE. *The French Student Uprising: November 1967–June 1968.* Trans. Maria Jolas. Boston: Beacon Press, 1971.

SCHULKIND, EUGENE (ED.). *The Paris Commune of 1871: The View from the Left.* New York: Grove Press, 1974.

SÉBEILLE, EDMOND. *L'Affaire Dominici.* Paris: Plon, 1970.

SHERMAN, LAWRENCE W., and THE NATIONAL COMMISSION ON HIGHER EDUCATION FOR POLICE OFFICERS. *The Quality of Police Education.* San Francisco, Washington, London: Jossey-Bass, 1978.

SICOT, MARCEL. *Servitude et Grandeur Policieres: Quarante Ans a la Sûreté.* Paris: Les Productions de Paris, 1959.

SOUCHON, HENRI. "Bertillon." In *Pioneers in Policing,* ed. Philip John Stead. Montclair, N.J.: Patterson Smith, 1977.

STANCIN, V.V. *La Criminalité a Paris.* Paris: Centre National de la Recherche Scientifique, 1968.

STEAD, PHILIP JOHN. *Vidocq: A Biography.* London: Staples, 1953.

———*The Police of Paris.* London: Staples, 1957.

————*Second Bureau*. London: Evans, 1959.

————*Le Deuxième Bureau sous l'Occupation*. Paris: Fayard, 1966.

————(ed.) *Pioneers in Policing*. Montclair, N.J.: Patterson Smith, 1977; Maidenhead, England: McGraw-Hill, 1977.

THORNTON, WILLIS. *The Liberation of Paris*. London: Rupert Hart-Davis, 1963.

TINT, HERBERT. *France since 1918*. New York and Evanston, Ill.: Harper and Row, 1970.

TOBIAS, J.J. "Police and Public in the United Kingdom." In *Police Forces in History*, ed. George L. Mosse. London, Beverley Hills: Sage, 1975.

TOURNIER, ALBERT. *Vadier, Président du Comité de la Sûreté Générale sous la Terreur*. Paris: Flammarion, n.d.

TULARD, JEAN. *La Préfecture de Police sous la Monarchie de Juillet*. Paris: Imprimerie Municipale, 1964.

VIDAL-NAQUET, PIERRE. *See* Schnapp, Alain.

WILLIAMS, ALAN. *The Police of Paris: 1718–1789*. Baton Rouge and London: Louisiana State University, 1979.

Index

171